Canary Islands A Traveler's Guide to Nature, Culture, and Adventure

Anna S. Vesper

Published by Travel The World, 2024.

CANARY ISLANDS A TRAVELER'S GUIDE TO NATURE, CULTURE, AND ADVENTURE

First edition. June 13, 2024.

Copyright © 2024 Anna S. Vesper.

ISBN: 979-8227659279

Written by Anna S. Vesper.

Chapter 1: Introduction to the Canary Islands

1.1 Overview and Significance

The Canary Islands, an enchanting archipelago located off the northwest coast of Africa, have long been a favored destination for travelers seeking diverse landscapes, vibrant culture, and a mild climate. Despite their proximity to the African continent, the Canary Islands are a part of Spain, providing a unique blend of Spanish and African influences that permeate their culture, cuisine, and lifestyle.

1.2 Geographical Layout

The Canary Islands consist of seven main islands: Tenerife, Gran Canaria, Lanzarote, Fuerteventura, La Palma, La Gomera, and El Hierro. Each island boasts its own distinct personality and charm, making the archipelago a versatile travel destination. Tenerife and Gran Canaria are the largest and most populous islands, known for their bustling cities, lively nightlife, and extensive amenities. Meanwhile, Lanzarote and Fuerteventura offer unique volcanic landscapes and pristine beaches, attracting nature lovers and water sports enthusiasts. The smaller islands, such as La Palma, La Gomera, and El Hierro, provide serene escapes with lush forests, rugged mountains, and tranquil villages.

1.3 Climate and Best Time to Visit

The Canary Islands enjoy a subtropical climate, often referred to as "eternal spring," characterized by mild temperatures year-round. Average temperatures range from 18°C (64°F) in the winter to 24°C (75°F) in the summer, making the islands a popular destination throughout the year. However, the best time to visit depends on individual preferences and activities planned.

For beach lovers and sun seekers, the summer months from June to September are ideal, offering warm temperatures and clear skies.

Winter, from December to February, is perfect for those looking to escape colder climates, with mild weather and fewer crowds. Spring and autumn, particularly April to May and October to November, are excellent times for outdoor activities such as hiking, with pleasant temperatures and blooming flora.

1.4 Historical Background

The history of the Canary Islands is a tapestry woven from the threads of indigenous cultures, European exploration, and colonial influences. The original inhabitants, known as the Guanches, were of Berber origin and lived on the islands for centuries before the arrival of the Spanish. The islands were officially claimed by Spain in the 15th century, marking the beginning of a new era of colonization and cultural fusion.

Throughout the centuries, the Canary Islands have served as a crucial stopover for explorers and traders crossing the Atlantic, significantly impacting their cultural and economic development. This historical significance is evident in the diverse architectural styles, culinary traditions, and local customs that travelers can experience today.

1.5 Cultural Richness

The culture of the Canary Islands is a vibrant blend of Spanish traditions and indigenous influences, enriched by the islands' strategic location as a crossroads between Europe, Africa, and the Americas. This cultural diversity is reflected in the islands' festivals, music, dance, and art.

One of the most notable cultural events is the Carnival of Santa Cruz de Tenerife, one of the largest and most spectacular carnivals in the world, featuring elaborate costumes, lively parades, and a festive atmosphere that attracts visitors from around the globe. Additionally, each island celebrates its own unique festivals and traditions, offering travelers a chance to immerse themselves in the local culture.

1.6 Natural Wonders

The Canary Islands are renowned for their stunning natural landscapes, shaped by volcanic activity and diverse ecosystems. The islands are home to four national parks, each offering unique geological formations and biodiversity.

Teide National Park in Tenerife, a UNESCO World Heritage site, is dominated by Mount Teide, the highest peak in Spain and an iconic symbol of the archipelago. The park's lunar-like landscape, with its striking rock formations and endemic flora, attracts hikers and nature enthusiasts.

In Lanzarote, Timanfaya National Park showcases the island's volcanic origins with its otherworldly lava fields and geothermal activity. The park offers guided tours that provide insight into the island's volcanic history and the resilience of its ecosystems.

Garajonay National Park in La Gomera, another UNESCO World Heritage site, is a verdant paradise with ancient laurel forests, misty valleys, and a rich diversity of plant and animal species. It is a haven for hikers and nature lovers seeking tranquility and natural beauty.

1.7 Practical Information for Travelers

Traveling to the Canary Islands is relatively straightforward, with numerous international flights connecting the islands to major cities in Europe and beyond. The two main airports, Tenerife South (TFS) and Gran Canaria (LPA), serve as the primary gateways to the archipelago, offering a wide range of flights and connections.

Once on the islands, travelers can easily explore the archipelago using a well-developed network of ferries and inter-island flights. Public transportation, including buses and taxis, is readily available, making it convenient to navigate both urban and rural areas. Additionally, car rentals are a popular option for those wishing to explore the islands at their own pace.

1.8 Accommodation Options

The Canary Islands offer a wide range of accommodation options to suit all budgets and preferences, from luxurious resorts and boutique hotels to budget-friendly hostels and vacation rentals. Travelers can choose from beachfront properties, charming rural retreats, and modern city hotels, ensuring a comfortable stay regardless of their travel style.

Many accommodations cater to specific interests, such as wellness retreats, family-friendly resorts, and eco-friendly lodges, allowing visitors to tailor their stay to their personal preferences and interests.

1.9 Culinary Delights

The culinary scene in the Canary Islands is a delightful reflection of the archipelago's diverse cultural heritage and abundant natural resources. Local cuisine is characterized by fresh seafood, locally grown produce, and traditional Spanish flavors, often accompanied by unique island twists.

Popular dishes include "papas arrugadas" (wrinkled potatoes) served with "mojo" sauces, grilled fish, and hearty stews such as "potaje de berros" (watercress soup). The islands also produce a variety of wines, particularly from Tenerife and Lanzarote, where volcanic soils impart distinct flavors to the grapes.

1.10 Sustainable Tourism

As awareness of environmental conservation grows, the Canary Islands have increasingly embraced sustainable tourism practices. Many initiatives focus on preserving the islands' natural beauty and cultural heritage while promoting responsible travel.

Travelers are encouraged to participate in eco-friendly activities, support local businesses, and minimize their environmental impact. This commitment to sustainability ensures that future generations can continue to enjoy the unique experiences and natural wonders of the Canary Islands.

Conclusion

The Canary Islands are a captivating destination that offers something for every traveler, from stunning landscapes and rich cultural heritage to modern amenities and diverse activities. Whether you're seeking adventure, relaxation, or cultural immersion, the Canary Islands provide an unforgettable travel experience. As we delve deeper into the individual islands and their unique offerings in the subsequent chapters, you'll discover why this archipelago continues to enchant and inspire visitors from around the world.

Chapter 2: Tenerife - The Island of Eternal Spring

2.1 Introduction to Tenerife

Tenerife, the largest of the Canary Islands, is often referred to as the "Island of Eternal Spring" due to its pleasant climate throughout the year. This island, with its diverse landscapes ranging from golden beaches to lush forests and towering mountains, attracts millions of visitors annually. Tenerife is a destination that caters to a wide array of interests, offering something for everyone, whether you are seeking adventure, relaxation, culture, or nature.

2.2 Getting There and Around

2.2.1 Arriving in Tenerife

Tenerife is served by two main airports: Tenerife South (Reina Sofía) Airport (TFS) and Tenerife North (Los Rodeos) Airport (TFN). Tenerife South Airport is the larger and busier of the two, handling most international flights, while Tenerife North Airport mainly deals with inter-island and domestic flights from mainland Spain. Numerous airlines offer direct flights to Tenerife from major cities across Europe, making it easily accessible for international travelers.

2.2.2 Transportation on the Island

Once you arrive, getting around Tenerife is straightforward. The island has a well-developed public transportation system, including buses operated by TITSA that cover most parts of the island. For more flexibility, many visitors opt to rent a car, which allows for easier exploration of more remote areas. Taxis are also readily available and reasonably priced.

2.3 Regions of Tenerife

Tenerife can be broadly divided into two main regions: the north and the south, each offering distinct experiences.

2.3.1 Northern Tenerife

The north of Tenerife is known for its lush landscapes, traditional towns, and a more laid-back atmosphere. Key attractions include:

Santa Cruz de Tenerife: The island's capital, known for its vibrant cultural scene, shopping, and the annual Carnival.

La Laguna: A UNESCO World Heritage site, this historic town boasts well-preserved colonial architecture and a lively student population.

Puerto de la Cruz: A popular resort town with beautiful botanical gardens and the renowned Loro Parque, a zoo and aquarium.

2.3.2 Southern Tenerife

The south of Tenerife is famous for its sunny weather, beautiful beaches, and bustling resorts. Highlights include:

Costa Adeje: A luxury resort area with upscale hotels, shopping centers, and sandy beaches.

Playa de las Américas: Known for its vibrant nightlife, this area is a hotspot for bars, clubs, and entertainment.

Los Cristianos: A more relaxed town with a charming harbor and excellent restaurants.

2.4 Natural Attractions

Tenerife is home to some of the most stunning natural attractions in the Canary Islands, offering numerous opportunities for outdoor activities.

2.4.1 Mount Teide National Park

Mount Teide, the highest peak in Spain, is the centerpiece of Teide National Park, a UNESCO World Heritage site. The park's unique volcanic landscape attracts hikers, nature lovers, and photographers. Visitors can take a cable car up to the summit for breathtaking views of the island and beyond. The park also offers several hiking trails of varying difficulty, showcasing the diverse flora and fauna of the region.

2.4.2 Anaga Rural Park

Located in the northeast of the island, Anaga Rural Park is a UNESCO Biosphere Reserve known for its ancient laurel forests, rugged mountains, and picturesque villages. The park is ideal for hiking, with well-marked trails that offer stunning vistas and a chance to experience the island's natural beauty up close.

2.4.3 Masca Valley

The Masca Valley, situated in the Teno Mountains, is one of Tenerife's hidden gems. The village of Masca is perched on a cliffside, surrounded by dramatic landscapes and deep ravines. The hike from Masca down to the coast is considered one of the most beautiful on the island, although it is challenging and requires a good level of fitness.

2.5 Beaches and Water Activities

Tenerife boasts a variety of beaches, ranging from golden sands to unique black volcanic beaches. Popular beaches include:

Playa de las Teresitas: Located near Santa Cruz, this man-made beach features golden sand imported from the Sahara Desert and is lined with palm trees.

Playa del Duque: Situated in Costa Adeje, this upscale beach offers calm waters, sun loungers, and excellent facilities.

Playa Jardín: Designed by the famous Canarian artist César Manrique, this black sand beach in Puerto de la Cruz is surrounded by beautiful gardens.

Water activities are abundant in Tenerife, including snorkeling, scuba diving, windsurfing, and paddleboarding. Whale and dolphin watching tours are also popular, with several companies offering excursions to see these magnificent creatures in their natural habitat.

2.6 Cultural Experiences

Tenerife offers a rich cultural heritage, with numerous opportunities to experience local traditions, music, and cuisine.

2.6.1 Festivals and Events

The Carnival of Santa Cruz de Tenerife is the island's most famous event, drawing thousands of visitors each year. This vibrant celebration features elaborate parades, costumes, music, and dancing. Other notable festivals include the Día de la Cruz in May and the Fiestas de San Andrés in November.

2.6.2 Museums and Historical Sites

Tenerife is home to several interesting museums and historical sites. The Museum of Nature and Archaeology in Santa Cruz offers insights into the island's natural history and the Guanche people. La Laguna's historic center, with its colonial architecture, is a must-visit for history enthusiasts.

2.6.3 Gastronomy

Tenerife's cuisine is a delicious blend of Spanish and local flavors. Must-try dishes include "papas arrugadas" with "mojo" sauce, fresh seafood, and "gofio," a traditional Canarian flour. The island also produces excellent wines, particularly from the regions of Tacoronte-Acentejo and Valle de La Orotava.

2.7 Adventure and Outdoor Activities

For adventure seekers, Tenerife offers a wide range of outdoor activities. Hiking, mountain biking, and paragliding are popular ways to explore the island's diverse landscapes. The coastline provides opportunities for surfing, kitesurfing, and deep-sea fishing.

2.8 Wellness and Relaxation

Tenerife is also a destination for wellness and relaxation. The island has numerous spas and wellness centers offering treatments that incorporate local ingredients such as aloe vera and volcanic stones. Yoga retreats and wellness resorts are available for those seeking a rejuvenating escape.

2.9 Family-Friendly Activities

Families will find plenty to do in Tenerife, with attractions such as Siam Park, one of the world's best water parks, and Loro Parque, a highly rated zoo and aquarium. The island's beaches are generally family-friendly, with calm waters and amenities catering to children.

2.10 Sustainable Tourism in Tenerife

Tenerife is committed to sustainable tourism practices, with efforts to preserve its natural beauty and cultural heritage. Visitors are encouraged to respect the environment, support local businesses, and participate in eco-friendly activities. Several eco-friendly accommodations and tour operators are available, promoting responsible travel.

Conclusion

Tenerife is a multifaceted destination that offers a perfect blend of natural beauty, cultural richness, and modern amenities. Whether you're seeking adventure, relaxation, or cultural immersion, Tenerife provides an unforgettable experience. As we continue to explore the Canary Islands in the following chapters, the unique charm and diversity of each island will further enhance your appreciation for this remarkable archipelago.

Chapter 3: Gran Canaria - A Continent in Miniature

3.1 Introduction to Gran Canaria

Gran Canaria, often described as a "continent in miniature," is the third-largest island in the Canary Islands archipelago and offers a remarkable variety of landscapes, climates, and experiences. From golden beaches and bustling cities to tranquil mountain villages and verdant forests, Gran Canaria's diversity makes it a must-visit destination for travelers. This chapter explores the island's unique features, attractions, and practical information to help you plan an unforgettable visit to Gran Canaria.

3.2 Getting There and Around

3.2.1 Arriving in Gran Canaria

Gran Canaria is served by Gran Canaria Airport (LPA), also known as Las Palmas Airport, which is the busiest airport in the Canary Islands. The airport offers numerous direct flights from major cities across Europe and is well-connected to other islands within the archipelago. Many international airlines, as well as low-cost carriers, operate frequent flights to and from Gran Canaria.

3.2.2 Transportation on the Island

Once on the island, getting around Gran Canaria is convenient and straightforward. The public bus system, operated by Global, provides extensive coverage across the island, including routes to major tourist areas and remote villages. Car rentals are also a popular choice, offering the freedom to explore the island at your own pace. Additionally, taxis are widely available and reasonably priced, especially for shorter trips within urban areas.

3.3 Regions of Gran Canaria

Gran Canaria can be divided into several distinct regions, each offering unique attractions and experiences.

3.3.1 Northern Gran Canaria

The northern part of Gran Canaria is characterized by its lush landscapes, historic towns, and cultural richness. Key attractions include:

Las Palmas de Gran Canaria: The island's capital and largest city, known for its vibrant cultural scene, historic districts like Vegueta and Triana, and beautiful beaches such as Las Canteras.

Arucas: Famous for its impressive neo-Gothic church, Iglesia de San Juan Bautista, and its rum distillery, where you can learn about the production of the local spirit.

Teror: A picturesque town with well-preserved colonial architecture, home to the Basilica of Nuestra Señora del Pino, a significant religious site.

3.3.2 Southern Gran Canaria

The southern part of Gran Canaria is renowned for its sunny weather, stunning beaches, and popular resorts. Highlights include:

Maspalomas: Known for its vast sand dunes, lighthouse, and lively nightlife. The Maspalomas Dunes are a protected nature reserve and a must-visit for their unique desert-like landscape.

Playa del Inglés: A bustling resort area with a wide range of accommodations, restaurants, bars, and entertainment options.

Puerto de Mogán: Often called "Little Venice," this charming fishing village features canals, colorful houses, and a beautiful marina.

3.3.3 Central Gran Canaria

The central region of Gran Canaria is a haven for nature lovers and outdoor enthusiasts, offering mountainous terrain, scenic hiking trails, and traditional villages. Key attractions include:

Roque Nublo: One of the island's most iconic natural landmarks, this massive volcanic rock formation provides stunning views and is accessible via a moderate hike.

Tejeda: A quaint mountain village known for its almond trees and traditional Canarian architecture, offering a glimpse into rural island life.

Cruz de Tejeda: A mountain pass and viewpoint, offering panoramic views of the surrounding landscapes and a starting point for several hiking trails.

3.4 Natural Attractions

Gran Canaria boasts a wealth of natural attractions, from dramatic volcanic landscapes to lush forests and pristine beaches.

3.4.1 Maspalomas Dunes

The Maspalomas Dunes, located in the south, are one of the island's most unique natural wonders. This protected area features rolling sand dunes, a lagoon, and a palm grove, creating a desert-like landscape that contrasts with the surrounding beach resorts. Visitors can explore the dunes on foot, take a camel ride, or simply relax on the nearby beaches.

3.4.2 Tamadaba Natural Park

Situated in the northwest of the island, Tamadaba Natural Park is a pristine area of natural beauty, characterized by dense pine forests, rugged cliffs, and breathtaking viewpoints. The park offers numerous hiking trails, camping areas, and opportunities for birdwatching and rock climbing.

3.4.3 Bandama Caldera

Bandama Caldera is a volcanic crater located near Las Palmas. The caldera, with a diameter of about 1 kilometer, is a fascinating geological site that offers excellent hiking opportunities. Visitors can hike down into the crater or enjoy the panoramic views from the Pico de Bandama, the highest point on the crater's rim.

3.5 Beaches and Water Activities

Gran Canaria is renowned for its diverse and beautiful beaches, catering to all types of beachgoers. Some of the most popular beaches include:

Playa de las Canteras: Located in Las Palmas, this urban beach is one of the best city beaches in Europe, offering golden sands, clear waters, and a vibrant promenade lined with restaurants and cafes.

Playa de Amadores: A family-friendly beach with calm waters, perfect for swimming and sunbathing. The beach is well-equipped with amenities, including sun loungers, parasols, and beachfront restaurants.

Playa de Güigüi: A remote and unspoiled beach on the west coast, accessible only by boat or a challenging hike. This secluded spot is ideal for those seeking tranquility and natural beauty.

Water activities are abundant in Gran Canaria, with options such as snorkeling, scuba diving, surfing, windsurfing, and jet skiing. The island's warm waters and diverse marine life make it a popular destination for underwater exploration.

3.6 Cultural Experiences

Gran Canaria's rich cultural heritage is reflected in its festivals, museums, and traditional towns.

3.6.1 Festivals and Events

Gran Canaria hosts numerous festivals throughout the year, celebrating everything from religious traditions to local culture. The Carnival of Las Palmas de Gran Canaria is one of the island's most famous events, featuring colorful parades, music, dancing, and elaborate costumes. Other notable festivals include the Fiesta de San Juan in June, marking the summer solstice with bonfires and fireworks, and the Fiestas del Charco in September, a unique celebration in the town of La Aldea de San Nicolás.

3.6.2 Museums and Historical Sites

Gran Canaria is home to several interesting museums and historical sites that offer insights into the island's history and culture. The Casa de Colón in Las Palmas is a museum dedicated to Christopher Columbus and his voyages, housed in a beautiful colonial building. The Cueva Pintada Museum and Archaeological Park in Gáldar features well-preserved cave paintings and artifacts from the island's pre-Hispanic past.

3.6.3 Gastronomy

The culinary scene in Gran Canaria is a delightful blend of traditional Canarian dishes and international influences. Must-try local dishes include "ropa vieja" (a stew made with chickpeas, meat, and vegetables), "sancocho" (a salted fish dish served with potatoes and "mojo" sauce), and "bienmesabe" (a dessert made with ground almonds, honey, and eggs). The island also produces excellent wines, particularly from the regions of Monte Lentiscal and El Monte.

3.7 Adventure and Outdoor Activities

Gran Canaria offers a wide range of outdoor activities for adventure seekers. The island's diverse landscapes provide excellent opportunities for hiking, mountain biking, and rock climbing. The coastal areas are ideal for water sports such as surfing, windsurfing, and kitesurfing. Paragliding and skydiving are also popular, offering thrilling experiences and stunning aerial views of the island.

3.8 Wellness and Relaxation

For those seeking relaxation and wellness, Gran Canaria has numerous spas, wellness centers, and yoga retreats. Many hotels and resorts offer spa facilities and wellness programs, incorporating local ingredients such as aloe vera and volcanic stones into their treatments. The island's natural beauty and tranquil environments make it an ideal destination for a rejuvenating getaway.

3.9 Family-Friendly Activities

Gran Canaria is a great destination for families, with a wide range of activities and attractions suitable for all ages. Popular family-friendly attractions include:

Aqualand Maspalomas: A large water park with slides, pools, and attractions for all ages.

Palmitos Park: A botanical garden and zoo featuring a variety of animals, bird shows, and beautiful landscapes.

Sioux City Park: A Wild West-themed park offering live shows, activities, and a glimpse into the Old West.

The island's beaches are generally family-friendly, with calm waters and facilities catering to children.

3.10 Sustainable Tourism in Gran Canaria

Gran Canaria is committed to promoting sustainable tourism practices, with efforts to preserve its natural landscapes and cultural heritage. Visitors are encouraged to participate in eco-friendly activities, support local businesses, and minimize their environmental impact. Several eco-friendly accommodations and tour operators are available, promoting responsible travel and environmental conservation.

Conclusion

Gran Canaria is a diverse and captivating destination that offers a perfect blend of natural beauty, cultural richness, and modern amenities. Whether you're seeking adventure, relaxation, or cultural immersion, Gran Canaria provides an unforgettable experience. As we continue to explore the Canary Islands in the following chapters, the unique charm and diversity of each island will further enhance your appreciation for this remarkable archipelago.

Chapter 4: Lanzarote - The Island of Fire

4.1 Introduction to Lanzarote

Lanzarote, often called the "Island of Fire," is renowned for its otherworldly landscapes shaped by volcanic activity. Located in the easternmost part of the Canary Islands, Lanzarote offers a unique combination of natural beauty, artistic influence, and sustainable tourism. This chapter delves into the island's distinct attractions, practical travel tips, and the essence of what makes Lanzarote a must-visit destination.

4.2 Getting There and Around

4.2.1 Arriving in Lanzarote

Lanzarote is served by César Manrique-Lanzarote Airport (ACE), located near the capital city, Arrecife. The airport handles numerous international flights from major European cities, making it easily accessible for travelers. Several airlines, including low-cost carriers, operate regular flights to Lanzarote, ensuring a range of options for visitors.

4.2.2 Transportation on the Island

Getting around Lanzarote is convenient, with various transportation options available. The public bus system, operated by Intercity Bus Lanzarote, covers major towns and tourist areas. Car rentals are popular for those who prefer the freedom to explore the island's diverse landscapes at their own pace. Taxis are also readily available and reasonably priced for shorter trips.

4.3 Regions of Lanzarote

Lanzarote can be divided into several regions, each offering distinct experiences and attractions.

4.3.1 Northern Lanzarote

The northern part of Lanzarote is known for its dramatic landscapes, charming villages, and artistic heritage. Key attractions include:

Haría: A picturesque village nestled in the Valley of a Thousand Palms, known for its traditional Canarian architecture and vibrant artisan market.

Jameos del Agua: An extraordinary cultural and tourist center created by César Manrique, featuring volcanic caves, an underground lake, and a unique auditorium.

Cueva de los Verdes: A fascinating lava tube that offers guided tours through its underground passages, showcasing the island's volcanic origins.

4.3.2 Southern Lanzarote

The southern part of the island is famous for its stunning beaches, luxury resorts, and volcanic landscapes. Highlights include:

Playa Blanca: A popular resort town with beautiful sandy beaches, a charming promenade, and excellent dining options.

Papagayo Beaches: A series of pristine, secluded beaches located within the Los Ajaches Natural Park, known for their crystal-clear waters and golden sands.

Timanfaya National Park: A UNESCO World Heritage site, this park features surreal volcanic landscapes and geothermal activity, offering visitors a glimpse into the island's fiery past.

4.3.3 Central Lanzarote

Central Lanzarote is the heart of the island, home to its capital, Arrecife, and several important cultural sites. Key attractions include:

Arrecife: The capital city, offering a blend of historical sites, shopping, and vibrant nightlife. Notable landmarks include the San Gabriel Castle and the Charco de San Ginés.

Fundación César Manrique: A museum and cultural center dedicated to the life and work of César Manrique, Lanzarote's most famous artist and architect.

La Geria: A unique wine-growing region where vines are cultivated in volcanic soil, producing distinctive wines. Visitors can tour local wineries and taste the island's celebrated Malvasía wines.

4.4 Natural Attractions

Lanzarote's natural beauty is characterized by its volcanic landscapes, pristine beaches, and unique flora and fauna.

4.4.1 Timanfaya National Park

Timanfaya National Park, often referred to as the "Fire Mountains," is a must-visit for anyone traveling to Lanzarote. The park's lunar-like landscape, shaped by volcanic eruptions in the 18th century, features craters, lava fields, and geothermal hotspots. Guided tours are available, providing insights into the park's geology and history. The El Diablo restaurant, designed by César Manrique, uses geothermal heat to cook food, offering a unique dining experience.

4.4.2 Los Hervideros

Located on the western coast, Los Hervideros is a series of dramatic cliffs and caves formed by lava flows meeting the ocean. The result is a stunning display of natural architecture, with waves crashing against the cliffs creating spectacular sprays and sounds. It's a great spot for photography and appreciating the raw power of nature.

4.4.3 El Golfo

El Golfo is a small village known for its striking green lagoon, El Lago Verde, formed in a volcanic crater. The vivid green color of the lagoon contrasts beautifully with the black sand beach and the surrounding red cliffs, making it a popular destination for visitors. The village itself offers charming restaurants with fresh seafood and stunning views of the Atlantic Ocean.

4.5 Beaches and Water Activities

Lanzarote boasts some of the most beautiful beaches in the Canary Islands, catering to a variety of preferences from family-friendly spots to secluded coves.

4.5.1 Playa de Papagayo

Playa de Papagayo, located in the Los Ajaches Natural Park, is considered one of the best beaches on the island. Its crystal-clear waters and golden sands make it perfect for swimming, snorkeling, and sunbathing. The beach is relatively secluded, offering a peaceful escape from more crowded areas.

4.5.2 Playa Famara

Playa Famara, on the northwest coast, is a long stretch of sandy beach backed by impressive cliffs. It's a favorite spot for surfers and kite surfers due to its consistent waves and strong winds. The nearby village of Caleta de Famara offers surf schools, equipment rentals, and cozy cafes.

4.5.3 Playa Flamingo

Located in Playa Blanca, Playa Flamingo is a family-friendly beach with calm waters and excellent facilities. The beach is protected by breakwaters, making it ideal for swimming and snorkeling. Sun loungers, parasols, and beachfront restaurants ensure a comfortable and enjoyable day by the sea.

4.6 Cultural Experiences

Lanzarote's rich cultural heritage is deeply influenced by the vision and work of César Manrique, whose legacy can be seen throughout the island.

4.6.1 César Manrique's Legacy

César Manrique, a renowned artist and architect, played a pivotal role in shaping Lanzarote's cultural and environmental identity. His commitment to sustainable development and integration of art with nature is evident in various attractions across the island. In addition to Jameos del Agua and the Fundación César Manrique, visitors can explore:

Mirador del Río: A stunning viewpoint designed by Manrique, offering panoramic views of the neighboring island of La Graciosa.

Cactus Garden (Jardín de Cactus): A beautifully landscaped garden featuring a vast collection of cacti and succulents, set within a former quarry.

4.6.2 Traditional Villages

Exploring Lanzarote's traditional villages provides a glimpse into the island's history and culture. Villages like Teguise, the former capital, offer charming streets lined with whitewashed houses, historic churches, and lively markets. Teguise's Sunday market is particularly popular, offering local crafts, food, and live music.

4.6.3 Gastronomy

Lanzarote's cuisine is a delightful blend of traditional Canarian flavors and innovative culinary techniques. Must-try dishes include:

Sancocho: A traditional fish stew served with potatoes, "mojo" sauce, and "gofio" (a type of flour made from roasted grains).

Bienmesabe: A delicious dessert made with ground almonds, honey, and eggs.

Lanzarote Wines: The island's unique volcanic soil produces exceptional wines, particularly the Malvasía grape variety. Visitors can enjoy wine tastings and tours in the La Geria region.

4.7 Adventure and Outdoor Activities

For adventure seekers, Lanzarote offers a wide range of outdoor activities that take advantage of its diverse landscapes.

4.7.1 Hiking

Lanzarote's volcanic terrain provides excellent opportunities for hiking. Popular trails include:

Caldera Blanca: A moderate hike that takes you to the rim of a large volcanic crater, offering stunning views of the surrounding landscape.

Ruta de los Volcanes: A scenic route through Timanfaya National Park, showcasing the island's dramatic volcanic scenery.

4.7.2 Cycling

Lanzarote is a popular destination for cycling enthusiasts, with its well-maintained roads and varied terrain. Whether you're a casual cyclist or a seasoned pro, the island offers routes to suit all levels. The annual Ironman Lanzarote competition is a testament to the island's popularity among athletes.

4.7.3 Water Sports

Lanzarote's coastal waters are ideal for a variety of water sports, including:

Surfing and Kite Surfing: Playa Famara and La Santa are top spots for catching waves and wind.

Scuba Diving: The island's clear waters and abundant marine life make it a prime location for diving, with numerous dive centers offering courses and excursions.

4.8 Wellness and Relaxation

Lanzarote's tranquil environment and natural beauty make it an ideal destination for wellness and relaxation. Many hotels and resorts offer spa services, wellness programs, and yoga retreats. The use of local ingredients, such as aloe vera and volcanic stones, in treatments enhances the experience.

4.9 Family-Friendly Activities

Families will find plenty to do in Lanzarote, with attractions catering to all ages. Highlights include:

Rancho Texas Lanzarote Park: A family-friendly theme park and zoo with live shows, water slides, and animal exhibits.

AquaLava Water Park: Located in Playa Blanca, this water park offers slides, pools, and attractions for kids and adults alike.

Submarine Safaris: An underwater adventure that allows families to explore the marine life of Lanzarote without getting wet.

4.10 Sustainable Tourism in Lanzarote

Lanzarote is a leader in sustainable tourism, thanks in large part to César Manrique's influence. The island has implemented numerous initiatives to preserve its natural environment and promote responsible travel. Visitors are encouraged to respect local ecosystems, support eco-friendly businesses, and participate in conservation efforts.

Conclusion

Lanzarote's unique landscapes, cultural richness, and commitment to sustainability make it a standout destination within the Canary

Islands. Whether you're exploring volcanic craters, relaxing on pristine beaches, or immersing yourself in the island's artistic heritage, Lanzarote offers an unforgettable travel experience. As we continue to explore the Canary Islands in the following chapters, the diverse offerings of each island will further illuminate the remarkable appeal of this archipelago.

Chapter 5: Fuerteventura - The Island of Winds

5.1 Introduction to Fuerteventura

Fuerteventura, known as the "Island of Winds," is the second-largest island in the Canary Islands archipelago. Famous for its extensive beaches, stunning sand dunes, and excellent conditions for water sports, Fuerteventura is a paradise for beach lovers and adventure enthusiasts alike. This chapter explores the island's unique attractions, practical travel tips, and the essence of what makes Fuerteventura a must-visit destination.

5.2 Getting There and Around

5.2.1 Arriving in Fuerteventura

Fuerteventura is served by Fuerteventura Airport (FUE), located near the capital, Puerto del Rosario. The airport handles numerous international and domestic flights, making it easily accessible for travelers. Many airlines, including low-cost carriers, operate regular flights to and from Fuerteventura, ensuring a variety of options for visitors.

5.2.2 Transportation on the Island

Getting around Fuerteventura is straightforward, with several transportation options available. The island has a reliable public bus system operated by Tiadhe, covering major towns and tourist areas. Car rentals are popular for those who want the freedom to explore the island's diverse landscapes at their own pace. Taxis are also readily available and reasonably priced for shorter trips.

5.3 Regions of Fuerteventura

Fuerteventura can be divided into several regions, each offering distinct experiences and attractions.

5.3.1 Northern Fuerteventura

The northern part of Fuerteventura is known for its beautiful beaches, charming villages, and vibrant tourism scene. Key attractions include:

Corralejo: A bustling resort town famous for its stunning sand dunes and lively nightlife. The Corralejo Natural Park features extensive sand dunes that stretch for miles, creating a desert-like landscape.

El Cotillo: A picturesque fishing village with beautiful beaches and a laid-back atmosphere. El Cotillo's beaches are known for their clear waters and excellent conditions for water sports.

La Oliva: A historical town with several interesting sites, including the Casa de los Coroneles, a well-preserved colonial mansion, and the Church of Our Lady of Candelaria.

5.3.2 Southern Fuerteventura

The southern part of the island is renowned for its expansive beaches and luxury resorts. Highlights include:

Jandía Peninsula: A popular tourist area with some of the best beaches on the island, including Playa de Sotavento and Playa de Cofete. The Jandía Natural Park offers stunning landscapes and diverse wildlife.

Morro Jable: A charming town with beautiful beaches, a picturesque harbor, and a variety of restaurants and shops. It's also a gateway to the Jandía Peninsula.

Costa Calma: Known for its tranquil beaches and upscale resorts, Costa Calma is a great destination for relaxation and water sports.

5.3.3 Central Fuerteventura

Central Fuerteventura is characterized by its rural landscapes, traditional villages, and cultural heritage. Key attractions include:

Betancuria: The island's former capital, Betancuria is a historical town with well-preserved colonial architecture, charming streets, and the Santa María Church. The Betancuria Rural Park offers beautiful landscapes and hiking opportunities.

Pájara: A quaint village known for its traditional Canarian architecture and the Church of Our Lady of Regla, which features unique Aztec-inspired decorations.

Antigua: Home to the Fuerteventura Cheese Museum, Antigua offers insights into the island's cheese-making tradition and the opportunity to taste local cheeses.

5.4 Natural Attractions

Fuerteventura's natural beauty is characterized by its extensive beaches, volcanic landscapes, and unique flora and fauna.

5.4.1 Corralejo Natural Park

Corralejo Natural Park, located in the north, is a must-visit for its vast sand dunes and stunning beaches. The park's dunes stretch for miles, creating a desert-like landscape that is perfect for exploring on foot. The beaches within the park are ideal for swimming, sunbathing, and water sports such as windsurfing and kitesurfing.

5.4.2 Jandía Natural Park

Jandía Natural Park, in the southern part of the island, offers diverse landscapes ranging from sandy beaches to rugged mountains. The park is home to Playa de Cofete, one of the most beautiful and remote beaches on the island. Hiking trails within the park provide opportunities to explore its unique flora and fauna, including the endangered Canary Island Egyptian vulture.

5.4.3 Islote de Lobos

Islote de Lobos, a small island located just off the coast of Corralejo, is a protected natural area that offers pristine beaches, clear waters, and excellent snorkeling opportunities. The island can be reached by a short ferry ride from Corralejo, and visitors can explore its hiking trails, lighthouse, and secluded coves.

5.5 Beaches and Water Activities

Fuerteventura is renowned for its extensive and beautiful beaches, catering to a variety of preferences from family-friendly spots to secluded coves.

5.5.1 Playa de Sotavento

Playa de Sotavento, located on the Jandía Peninsula, is one of the most famous beaches on the island. Its long stretch of golden sand and shallow, clear waters make it perfect for swimming, sunbathing, and water sports. The beach is particularly popular with windsurfers and kitesurfers due to its consistent winds and excellent conditions.

5.5.2 Playa de Cofete

Playa de Cofete is a remote and unspoiled beach on the western coast of the Jandía Peninsula. Accessible via a challenging dirt road, the beach offers a sense of isolation and natural beauty that is hard to find elsewhere. The dramatic scenery, with its rugged mountains and vast expanse of sand, makes it a favorite among nature lovers and photographers.

5.5.3 Playa de Esquinzo

Playa de Esquinzo, located near Costa Calma, is a quieter beach that offers calm waters and a relaxed atmosphere. It's a great spot for families and those looking to escape the busier tourist areas. The beach is well-equipped with amenities, including sun loungers, parasols, and beachfront restaurants.

5.6 Cultural Experiences

Fuerteventura's rich cultural heritage is reflected in its festivals, museums, and traditional towns.

5.6.1 Festivals and Events

Fuerteventura hosts several festivals throughout the year, celebrating local culture, music, and traditions. The Fuerteventura Carnival, held in various towns across the island, features colorful parades, music, and dancing. The Festival of San Juan in June is marked by bonfires and fireworks, celebrating the summer solstice. The International Kite Festival, held annually in Corralejo, attracts kite enthusiasts from around the world to display their creations on the island's beaches.

5.6.2 Museums and Historical Sites

Fuerteventura is home to several interesting museums and historical sites that offer insights into the island's history and culture. The Betancuria Archaeological Museum showcases artifacts from the island's pre-Hispanic past, while the Ecomuseum of La Alcogida in Tefía provides a glimpse into traditional rural life on the island. The Salt Museum in Las Salinas del Carmen explores the history and production of salt on Fuerteventura.

5.6.3 Gastronomy

Fuerteventura's cuisine is a delightful blend of traditional Canarian dishes and fresh local ingredients. Must-try dishes include:

Gofio: A traditional Canarian flour made from roasted grains, often used in soups, stews, and desserts.

Majorero Cheese: A type of goat cheese produced on the island, known for its rich flavor and creamy texture. The island's cheese-making tradition is celebrated at the Fuerteventura Cheese Museum in Antigua.

Sancocho: A traditional fish stew served with potatoes, "mojo" sauce, and "gofio."

5.7 Adventure and Outdoor Activities

Fuerteventura offers a wide range of outdoor activities for adventure seekers, taking advantage of its diverse landscapes and excellent conditions for water sports.

5.7.1 Water Sports

Fuerteventura's consistent winds and clear waters make it a paradise for water sports enthusiasts. Popular activities include:

Windsurfing and Kitesurfing: The island's beaches, particularly Playa de Sotavento and Playa de Corralejo, offer excellent conditions for windsurfing and kitesurfing, with several schools and rental shops available.

Surfing: The north coast, including spots like El Cotillo and La Pared, provides some of the best surfing conditions in the Canary Islands, with waves suitable for all levels.

Scuba Diving and Snorkeling: The island's clear waters and diverse marine life make it a popular destination for diving and snorkeling, with numerous dive centers offering courses and excursions.

5.7.2 Hiking and Cycling

Fuerteventura's varied terrain offers excellent opportunities for hiking and cycling. Popular trails include:

Pico de la Zarza: The highest point on the island, offering panoramic views of the Jandía Peninsula and the surrounding landscapes. The hike to the summit is challenging but rewarding.

GR 131: A long-distance hiking trail that traverses the island from north to south, providing a comprehensive experience of Fuerteventura's diverse landscapes.

Lobos Island: The small island off the coast of Corralejo offers several hiking trails, including a route to the lighthouse and around the volcanic crater.

5.8 Wellness and Relaxation

Fuerteventura's tranquil environment and natural beauty make it an ideal destination for wellness and relaxation. Many hotels and resorts offer spa services, wellness programs, and yoga retreats. The island's natural elements, such as aloe vera and volcanic stones, are often incorporated into treatments, enhancing the experience.

5.9 Family-Friendly Activities

Families will find plenty to do in Fuerteventura, with attractions catering to all ages. Highlights include:

Oasis Park: A large zoo and botanical garden in La Lajita, featuring a wide variety of animals, live shows, and beautiful gardens. The park also offers camel rides and a petting zoo.

Acua Water Park: Located in Corralejo, this water park offers slides, pools, and attractions for kids and adults alike.

Dinosaur Park: An interactive park in La Lajita where children can learn about dinosaurs and prehistoric life through exhibits and activities.

The island's beaches are generally family-friendly, with calm waters and facilities catering to children.

5.10 Sustainable Tourism in Fuerteventura

Fuerteventura is committed to promoting sustainable tourism practices, with efforts to preserve its natural landscapes and cultural heritage. Visitors are encouraged to participate in eco-friendly activities, support local businesses, and minimize their environmental impact. Several eco-friendly accommodations and tour operators are available, promoting responsible travel and environmental conservation.

Conclusion

Fuerteventura's extensive beaches, stunning landscapes, and excellent conditions for water sports make it a standout destination within the Canary Islands. Whether you're seeking adventure, relaxation, or cultural immersion, Fuerteventura offers an unforgettable travel experience. As we continue to explore the Canary Islands in the following chapters, the diverse offerings of each island will further illuminate the remarkable appeal of this archipelago.

Chapter 6: La Palma - La Isla Bonita

6.1 Introduction to La Palma

La Palma, often referred to as "La Isla Bonita" (The Beautiful Island), is known for its lush landscapes, rich biodiversity, and dramatic volcanic terrain. As one of the lesser-visited islands in the Canary archipelago, La Palma offers a serene and unspoiled environment, making it a perfect destination for nature lovers, hikers, and stargazers. This chapter explores La Palma's unique attractions, practical travel tips, and the elements that contribute to its enchanting allure.

6.2 Getting There and Around

6.2.1 Arriving in La Palma

La Palma is served by La Palma Airport (SPC), located near the capital city, Santa Cruz de La Palma. The airport handles a mix of international and domestic flights, including connections from mainland Spain and other Canary Islands. Several airlines, including low-cost carriers, operate regular flights to and from La Palma, making it accessible for travelers.

6.2.2 Transportation on the Island

Navigating La Palma is relatively easy with various transportation options available. The island's public bus system, operated by Transportes Insular La Palma (TILP), covers major towns and tourist areas. However, for more flexibility and to reach remote hiking trails and scenic spots, renting a car is highly recommended. Taxis are also available and can be a convenient option for shorter trips.

6.3 Regions of La Palma

La Palma can be divided into several regions, each offering distinct experiences and attractions.

6.3.1 Eastern La Palma

The eastern part of La Palma is known for its cultural and historical significance, as well as its lush green landscapes. Key attractions include:

Santa Cruz de La Palma: The island's capital and largest city, known for its well-preserved colonial architecture, charming streets, and vibrant cultural scene. Notable landmarks include the 16th-century Church of El Salvador and the Naval Museum, housed in a replica of Columbus's ship, the Santa Maria.

San Andrés y Sauces: A picturesque town surrounded by banana plantations and laurel forests. Nearby attractions include the Charco Azul natural pools and the Los Tilos Forest, a UNESCO Biosphere Reserve with lush greenery and scenic hiking trails.

Breña Baja: A municipality known for its traditional architecture, beautiful gardens, and stunning viewpoints such as Mirador de la Cumbrecita.

6.3.2 Western La Palma

The western part of the island is characterized by its dramatic volcanic landscapes and excellent stargazing opportunities. Highlights include:

Los Llanos de Aridane: The largest municipality on the island, known for its bustling town center, colorful houses, and proximity to natural attractions like the Caldera de Taburiente National Park.

El Paso: A town located in the heart of the island, offering access to the Caldera de Taburiente National Park and the Cumbrecita viewpoint. El Paso is also known for its silk-making tradition and the Silk Museum.

Tazacorte: A coastal town with beautiful black sand beaches and a charming harbor. Tazacorte is famous for its mild climate and lush banana plantations.

6.3.3 Northern La Palma

Northern La Palma is renowned for its rugged terrain, remote villages, and scenic viewpoints. Key attractions include:

Garafía: A municipality known for its dramatic cliffs, ancient dragon trees, and the Roque de los Muchachos Observatory, one of the world's leading astronomical observatories.

Barlovento: A town surrounded by forests and agricultural terraces. Nearby attractions include the La Laguna de Barlovento reservoir and the scenic Cubo de la Galga hiking trail.

Puntagorda: A village known for its almond blossoms and stunning viewpoints such as Mirador de Miraflores and Mirador de El Time.

6.4 Natural Attractions

La Palma's natural beauty is characterized by its volcanic landscapes, lush forests, and pristine beaches.

6.4.1 Caldera de Taburiente National Park

Caldera de Taburiente National Park is one of La Palma's most iconic natural attractions. The park features a massive volcanic crater, dense forests, and numerous hiking trails that offer breathtaking views of the island's rugged terrain. The Barranco de las Angustias trail leads into the heart of the caldera, passing through lush vegetation, waterfalls, and streams.

6.4.2 Roque de los Muchachos

Roque de los Muchachos is the highest point on La Palma, offering stunning panoramic views of the island and beyond. The area is home to the Roque de los Muchachos Observatory, one of the world's premier astronomical observatories. The clear, dark skies of La Palma make it an ideal location for stargazing, and several guided tours and visitor centers provide insights into the island's astronomical significance.

6.4.3 Los Tilos Forest

Los Tilos Forest, located near San Andrés y Sauces, is a lush laurel forest that is part of the UNESCO Biosphere Reserve. The forest features numerous hiking trails, including the popular Cascada de los Tilos trail, which leads to a beautiful waterfall. The Visitor Center provides information about the forest's biodiversity and conservation efforts.

6.5 Beaches and Water Activities

While La Palma is not as famous for its beaches as some other Canary Islands, it still offers several beautiful and unique coastal spots.

6.5.1 Playa de Puerto Naos

Playa de Puerto Naos, located on the western coast, is one of La Palma's most popular beaches. The beach features black volcanic sand, clear waters, and excellent facilities, including sun loungers, parasols, and beachfront restaurants. It is a great spot for swimming, sunbathing, and snorkeling.

6.5.2 Playa de Los Cancajos

Playa de Los Cancajos, situated near the capital, Santa Cruz de La Palma, is another popular beach with black sand and calm waters. The beach is well-equipped with amenities and offers good conditions for swimming and snorkeling. The nearby coastal promenade is perfect for a leisurely stroll, offering stunning views of the Atlantic Ocean.

6.5.3 Charco Azul

Charco Azul, located near San Andrés y Sauces, is a series of natural swimming pools created by volcanic rock formations. The clear, calm waters make it an ideal spot for swimming and relaxing. The area is equipped with sunbathing platforms, changing facilities, and picnic areas, making it a perfect destination for a family day out.

6.6 Cultural Experiences

La Palma's rich cultural heritage is reflected in its festivals, museums, and traditional towns.

6.6.1 Festivals and Events

La Palma hosts several festivals throughout the year, celebrating local culture, music, and traditions. The Bajada de la Virgen de las Nieves, held every five years in Santa Cruz de La Palma, is one of the island's most significant events. The festival features religious processions, music, dance, and traditional performances. Other notable festivals include the Día de Los Indianos, a unique carnival event in Santa Cruz de La Palma, and the Fiesta del Almendro en Flor, celebrating the almond blossom season in Puntagorda.

6.6.2 Museums and Historical Sites

La Palma is home to several interesting museums and historical sites that offer insights into the island's history and culture. The Insular Museum in Santa Cruz de La Palma, housed in a former Franciscan convent, features exhibits on the island's natural history, archaeology, and art. The Silk Museum in El Paso showcases the traditional silk-making process, which has been preserved on the island for centuries. The La Zarza Archaeological Park in Garafía features ancient petroglyphs and provides information about the island's indigenous inhabitants.

6.6.3 Gastronomy

La Palma's cuisine is a delightful blend of traditional Canarian dishes and fresh local ingredients. Must-try dishes include:

Papas Arrugadas: Small, wrinkled potatoes served with "mojo" sauce, a staple of Canarian cuisine.

Sancocho Canario: A traditional fish stew served with potatoes, sweet potatoes, and "mojo" sauce.

Bienmesabe: A delicious dessert made with ground almonds, honey, and eggs.

La Palma is also known for its locally produced wines, particularly from the regions of Tijarafe and Fuencaliente. Visitors can enjoy wine tastings and tours at local wineries, sampling the island's unique volcanic wines.

6.7 Adventure and Outdoor Activities

For adventure seekers, La Palma offers a wide range of outdoor activities that take advantage of its diverse landscapes.

6.7.1 Hiking

La Palma is renowned for its excellent hiking trails, offering a variety of routes for all levels of experience. Popular trails include:

Ruta de los Volcanes: A challenging trail that traverses the volcanic ridge of the island, offering stunning views of the craters and surrounding landscapes.

Camino Real de la Costa: A coastal path that connects several villages and offers beautiful views of the Atlantic Ocean and the rugged coastline.

Barranco de las Angustias: A scenic trail that leads into the Caldera de Taburiente, passing through lush vegetation, waterfalls, and streams.

6.7.2 Cycling

La Palma's varied terrain provides excellent opportunities for cycling, with routes ranging from coastal roads to challenging mountain climbs. The island's quiet roads and scenic landscapes make it a popular destination for both road cycling and mountain biking.

6.7.3 Paragliding

The island's dramatic landscapes and favorable weather conditions make it an ideal location for paragliding. Several companies offer tandem flights, allowing visitors to experience the thrill of soaring above La Palma's stunning scenery.

6.8 Wellness and Relaxation

La Palma's tranquil environment and natural beauty make it an ideal destination for wellness and relaxation. Many hotels and resorts offer spa services, wellness programs, and yoga retreats. The island's natural elements, such as aloe vera and volcanic stones, are often incorporated into treatments, enhancing the experience.

6.9 Family-Friendly Activities

Families will find plenty to do in La Palma, with attractions catering to all ages. Highlights include:

Maroparque: A small zoo and botanical garden located near Santa Cruz de La Palma, featuring a variety of animals, birds, and plants. The park offers a fun and educational experience for children and adults alike.

La Palma Aquarium: Located in the capital, this aquarium showcases the diverse marine life of the Canary Islands, with interactive exhibits and touch tanks for kids.

Natural Swimming Pools: Charco Azul and La Fajana are family-friendly natural pools with calm waters, perfect for swimming and relaxing.

6.10 Sustainable Tourism in La Palma

La Palma is committed to promoting sustainable tourism practices, with efforts to preserve its natural landscapes and cultural heritage. Visitors are encouraged to participate in eco-friendly activities, support local businesses, and minimize their environmental impact. Several eco-friendly accommodations and tour operators are available, promoting responsible travel and environmental conservation.

Conclusion

La Palma's lush landscapes, rich biodiversity, and serene environment make it a standout destination within the Canary Islands. Whether you're seeking adventure, relaxation, or cultural immersion, La Palma offers an unforgettable travel experience. As we continue to explore the Canary Islands in the following chapters, the diverse offerings of each island will further illuminate the remarkable appeal of this archipelago.

Chapter 7: La Gomera - The Magic Island

7.1 Introduction to La Gomera

La Gomera, known as the "Magic Island," is a small, circular island in the Canary archipelago celebrated for its lush landscapes, deep ravines, and ancient laurel forests. This island is a haven for hikers, nature enthusiasts, and those seeking a tranquil retreat away from the hustle and bustle of more tourist-heavy destinations. La Gomera's unique culture, historical significance, and natural beauty make it a must-visit destination. This chapter explores La Gomera's key attractions, practical travel tips, and the elements that contribute to its mystical charm.

7.2 Getting There and Around

7.2.1 Arriving in La Gomera

La Gomera is accessible by ferry and by air. The island has a small airport, La Gomera Airport (GMZ), located near Playa Santiago, which primarily handles inter-island flights from Tenerife. Most visitors, however, arrive via ferry from Tenerife. Ferries depart from Los Cristianos in Tenerife to San Sebastián de La Gomera, the island's capital, several times a day. The ferry ride takes approximately 50 minutes to an hour.

7.2.2 Transportation on the Island

Getting around La Gomera can be achieved through several transportation options. The island's public bus system, operated by GuaguaGomera, covers major towns and tourist areas, but the service is limited compared to larger islands. For more flexibility, especially for exploring remote hiking trails and scenic spots, renting a car is highly recommended. Taxis are available but can be more costly for longer trips.

7.3 Regions of La Gomera

La Gomera can be divided into several regions, each offering distinct experiences and attractions.

7.3.1 Eastern La Gomera

The eastern part of La Gomera includes the capital and several charming villages. Key attractions include:

San Sebastián de La Gomera: The island's capital and main port, known for its historical sites related to Christopher Columbus, who stopped here on his way to the New World. Notable landmarks include the Torre del Conde, a medieval fortress, and the Church of the Assumption.

Hermigua: A picturesque valley known for its banana plantations, lush greenery, and the Ethnographic Museum, which offers insights into the island's traditional way of life.

Agulo: Often called the "Pearl of La Gomera," this village features well-preserved colonial architecture, cobbled streets, and stunning views of the Atlantic Ocean and Mount Teide on Tenerife.

7.3.2 Western La Gomera

The western part of the island is characterized by its rugged terrain, dramatic coastlines, and tranquil villages. Highlights include:

Valle Gran Rey: A popular tourist area known for its terraced hillsides, palm groves, and beautiful beaches such as Playa del Inglés and Playa de Valle Gran Rey. The valley is a favorite spot for hiking, swimming, and enjoying sunset views.

Alojera: A small, traditional village famous for its production of palm honey, a local delicacy made from the sap of palm trees. The nearby beach, Playa de Alojera, offers a peaceful escape.

Chipude: One of the oldest settlements on the island, Chipude is known for its ancient archaeological sites and the impressive Fortaleza de Chipude, a flat-topped mountain offering panoramic views.

7.3.3 Northern La Gomera

Northern La Gomera is known for its dramatic landscapes, lush vegetation, and remote villages. Key attractions include:

Vallehermoso: The largest municipality on the island, Vallehermoso is surrounded by stunning scenery, including the iconic

Roque Cano rock formation. The village is a great base for exploring the island's hiking trails.

Agulo: In addition to being a highlight of eastern La Gomera, Agulo is easily accessible from the north and offers breathtaking views and charming streets.

Garajonay National Park: A UNESCO World Heritage site that covers much of the island's interior, featuring ancient laurel forests, diverse flora and fauna, and numerous hiking trails.

7.4 Natural Attractions

La Gomera's natural beauty is characterized by its dramatic terrain, dense forests, and unique geological formations.

7.4.1 Garajonay National Park

Garajonay National Park is the crown jewel of La Gomera's natural attractions. The park, a UNESCO World Heritage site, is home to ancient laurel forests that are remnants of the prehistoric forests that once covered much of Southern Europe. The park's lush greenery, mist-covered trees, and diverse plant species create an otherworldly atmosphere. Popular trails include the Alto de Garajonay, the highest point on the island, and the El Cedro forest, known for its dense vegetation and scenic waterfalls.

7.4.2 Los Roques

Los Roques are a series of impressive rock formations scattered across La Gomera, with the most famous being Roque de Agando. These volcanic plugs are remnants of ancient volcanic activity and offer stunning viewpoints over the island's rugged landscape. The Roque de Agando viewpoint is easily accessible by car and provides panoramic views of the surrounding valleys and mountains.

7.4.3 Valle Gran Rey

Valle Gran Rey, located on the western coast, is known for its dramatic terraced hillsides, palm groves, and beautiful beaches. The valley is a popular destination for hikers, offering numerous trails that lead through lush vegetation and picturesque villages. The area is also famous for its stunning sunsets, best enjoyed from the beach or one of the many viewpoints.

7.5 Beaches and Water Activities

While La Gomera is not primarily known for its beaches, it offers several beautiful and secluded coastal spots.

7.5.1 Playa de Santiago

Playa de Santiago, located near the airport and the town of Alajeró, is one of the island's most popular beaches. The beach features black volcanic sand, clear waters, and excellent facilities, including sun loungers, parasols, and beachfront restaurants. It's a great spot for swimming, sunbathing, and enjoying local seafood.

7.5.2 Playa de Valle Gran Rey

Playa de Valle Gran Rey, situated in the western part of the island, is a series of beautiful beaches that cater to different preferences. Playa del Inglés is known for its dramatic cliffs and strong waves, making it ideal for experienced swimmers and surfers. Playa de Vueltas, on the other hand, offers calm waters and a relaxed atmosphere, perfect for families and sunbathers.

7.5.3 Playa de La Caleta

Playa de La Caleta, located near Hermigua, is a secluded beach with black sand and clear waters. The beach is surrounded by dramatic cliffs and offers a peaceful escape from more crowded areas. It is a great spot for swimming, snorkeling, and enjoying the natural beauty of La Gomera.

7.6 Cultural Experiences

La Gomera's rich cultural heritage is reflected in its unique traditions, festivals, and historical sites.

7.6.1 Festivals and Events

La Gomera hosts several festivals throughout the year, celebrating local culture, music, and traditions. The Bajada de la Virgen de Guadalupe, held every five years, is one of the island's most significant events. The festival involves a procession from Puntallana to San

Sebastián de La Gomera, accompanied by traditional music and dance. Other notable festivals include the Fiesta de San Juan in June, marked by bonfires and fireworks, and the Fiesta de Nuestra Señora de la Candelaria in February.

7.6.2 Museums and Historical Sites

La Gomera is home to several interesting museums and historical sites that offer insights into the island's history and culture. The Archaeological Museum of La Gomera, located in San Sebastián, features exhibits on the island's indigenous inhabitants and their way of life. The Torre del Conde, a medieval fortress in the capital, provides a glimpse into the island's colonial past. Additionally, the island's numerous churches, such as the Church of the Assumption in San Sebastián, showcase beautiful architecture and religious art.

7.6.3 Silbo Gomero

Silbo Gomero, the island's unique whistled language, is a fascinating cultural tradition that has been recognized by UNESCO as an Intangible Cultural Heritage. Developed by the island's early inhabitants to communicate across its deep ravines and valleys, Silbo Gomero is still taught in schools and practiced today. Visitors can learn about this unique form of communication at various cultural centers and demonstrations across the island.

7.7 Adventure and Outdoor Activities

For adventure seekers, La Gomera offers a wide range of outdoor activities that take advantage of its diverse landscapes.

7.7.1 Hiking

La Gomera is a hiker's paradise, with an extensive network of trails that traverse its varied terrain. Popular trails include:

El Cedro to Hermigua: A scenic trail that passes through the lush El Cedro forest and offers stunning views of the surrounding valleys and mountains.

Roque de Agando: A challenging hike that leads to one of the island's most iconic rock formations, offering panoramic views of the landscape.

Valle Gran Rey: Numerous trails wind through the valley's terraced hillsides, palm groves, and picturesque villages, providing a diverse hiking experience.

7.7.2 Cycling

La Gomera's varied terrain provides excellent opportunities for cycling, with routes ranging from coastal roads to challenging mountain climbs. The island's quiet roads and scenic landscapes make it a popular destination for both road cycling and mountain biking.

7.7.3 Water Sports

While La Gomera is not as well-known for water sports as some other Canary Islands, it still offers opportunities for activities such as snorkeling, diving, and kayaking. The island's clear waters and diverse marine life make it a great destination for underwater exploration.

7.8 Wellness and Relaxation

La Gomera's tranquil environment and natural beauty make it an ideal destination for wellness and relaxation. Many hotels and resorts offer spa services, wellness programs, and yoga retreats. The island's natural elements, such as aloe vera and volcanic stones, are often incorporated into treatments, enhancing the experience.

7.9 Family-Friendly Activities

Families will find plenty to do in La Gomera, with attractions catering to all ages. Highlights include:

Valle Gran Rey Beaches: The beaches in Valle Gran Rey, such as Playa de Vueltas, offer calm waters and a relaxed atmosphere, perfect for families with children.

Garajonay National Park: The park's numerous trails and scenic viewpoints provide a great outdoor experience for families. The El Cedro forest, with its lush vegetation and waterfalls, is particularly popular with children.

Los Organos: A unique rock formation on the northern coast that resembles organ pipes. Boat tours are available to view this natural wonder from the sea, providing a fun and educational experience for families.

7.10 Sustainable Tourism in La Gomera

La Gomera is committed to promoting sustainable tourism practices, with efforts to preserve its natural landscapes and cultural heritage. Visitors are encouraged to participate in eco-friendly activities, support local businesses, and minimize their environmental impact. Several eco-friendly accommodations and tour operators are available, promoting responsible travel and environmental conservation.

Conclusion

La Gomera's lush landscapes, rich cultural heritage, and serene environment make it a standout destination within the Canary Islands. Whether you're seeking adventure, relaxation, or cultural immersion, La Gomera offers an unforgettable travel experience. As we continue to explore the Canary Islands in the following chapters, the diverse offerings of each island will further illuminate the remarkable appeal of this archipelago.

Chapter 8: El Hierro - The Meridian Island

8.1 Introduction to El Hierro

El Hierro, the smallest and most remote of the Canary Islands, is often referred to as the "Meridian Island" because it was once considered the westernmost point of the known world. This unspoiled island is a UNESCO Biosphere Reserve, known for its rugged landscapes, pristine waters, and commitment to sustainable development. El Hierro is a paradise for nature lovers, divers, and those seeking an off-the-beaten-path experience. This chapter explores El Hierro's unique attractions, practical travel tips, and the elements that make it a hidden gem in the Canary Islands.

8.2 Getting There and Around

8.2.1 Arriving in El Hierro

El Hierro is accessible by air and sea. The island has a small airport, El Hierro Airport (VDE), located near Valverde, the capital. The airport primarily handles inter-island flights from Tenerife and Gran Canaria. For those traveling by sea, ferries operate between Los Cristianos in Tenerife and the port of La Estaca in El Hierro. The ferry ride takes approximately 2.5 hours.

8.2.2 Transportation on the Island

Getting around El Hierro is best achieved by renting a car, as public transportation options are limited. The island's road network is well-maintained and provides access to its major attractions. Taxis are available but can be more expensive for longer journeys. For those who prefer not to drive, guided tours are a convenient option to explore the island.

8.3 Regions of El Hierro

El Hierro can be divided into several regions, each offering distinct experiences and attractions.

8.3.1 Northern El Hierro

The northern part of El Hierro is characterized by its lush forests, rugged coastlines, and traditional villages. Key attractions include:

Valverde: The capital of El Hierro, Valverde is a charming town with narrow streets, traditional Canarian architecture, and a relaxed atmosphere. Notable sites include the Church of Santa María de la Concepción and the Ethnographic Museum.

El Golfo Valley: A lush, green valley surrounded by dramatic cliffs and home to several picturesque villages such as Frontera and Tigaday. The valley is known for its vineyards and fruit orchards.

Pozo de la Salud: A natural spa with mineral-rich waters believed to have therapeutic properties. The spa offers a range of treatments and is a popular spot for relaxation and wellness.

8.3.2 Southern El Hierro

The southern part of the island is known for its volcanic landscapes, stunning viewpoints, and unique cultural sites. Highlights include:

La Restinga: A small fishing village and the southernmost point of El Hierro. La Restinga is renowned for its excellent diving spots and marine reserve, offering some of the best diving in Europe.

El Pinar: A picturesque village surrounded by pine forests and vineyards. El Pinar is known for its traditional crafts, including pottery and weaving.

Mirador de la Peña: A viewpoint designed by César Manrique, offering breathtaking views of the El Golfo Valley and the Atlantic Ocean. The on-site restaurant provides a perfect spot to enjoy the scenery while sampling local cuisine.

8.3.3 Western El Hierro

Western El Hierro is characterized by its rugged terrain, ancient landscapes, and remote beauty. Key attractions include:

Faro de Orchilla: The westernmost point of the island, marked by the Orchilla Lighthouse. This spot was historically considered the "end of the world" and the prime meridian before Greenwich.

El Sabinar: A unique forest of ancient, wind-sculpted juniper trees that have been twisted into surreal shapes by the island's strong winds. The forest offers a fascinating landscape for photography and exploration.

La Dehesa: Home to the revered Virgen de los Reyes, the patron saint of El Hierro. The sanctuary is a pilgrimage site, and the surrounding area offers beautiful hiking trails and scenic views.

8.4 Natural Attractions

El Hierro's natural beauty is characterized by its volcanic landscapes, clear waters, and diverse ecosystems.

8.4.1 La Frontera Rural Park

La Frontera Rural Park encompasses much of the northern and western parts of El Hierro, featuring a mix of volcanic terrain, lush forests, and coastal cliffs. The park offers numerous hiking trails, such as the Camino de Jinama, which provides stunning views of the El Golfo Valley and the Atlantic Ocean.

8.4.2 El Hierro Marine Reserve

The El Hierro Marine Reserve, located near La Restinga, is a protected area renowned for its rich marine biodiversity and excellent diving conditions. The reserve features underwater volcanic formations, vibrant coral reefs, and an abundance of marine life, making it a top destination for scuba divers and snorkelers.

8.4.3 El Julan

El Julan is an archaeological site on the southern slopes of El Hierro, featuring ancient petroglyphs created by the island's indigenous Bimbache people. The site includes a visitor center that provides insights into the history and culture of El Hierro's early inhabitants. Guided tours are available to explore the petroglyphs and learn about their significance.

8.5 Beaches and Water Activities

El Hierro offers several beautiful and secluded beaches, as well as excellent opportunities for water activities.

8.5.1 Playa de Tacorón

Playa de Tacorón, located near La Restinga, is a small, picturesque beach with red sand and crystal-clear waters. The beach is ideal for swimming, snorkeling, and relaxing, offering a tranquil escape from more crowded spots. The nearby volcanic cliffs provide a stunning backdrop.

8.5.2 Playa del Verodal

Playa del Verodal, situated on the western coast, is a striking beach with reddish sand and dramatic cliffs. The beach is known for its rugged beauty and strong waves, making it a popular spot for surfers. However, caution is advised when swimming due to the strong currents.

8.5.3 Charco Azul

Charco Azul, located in the El Golfo Valley, is a series of natural pools formed by volcanic rock. The clear, calm waters make it a perfect spot for swimming and snorkeling. The surrounding cliffs and lush vegetation create a beautiful and serene setting.

8.6 Cultural Experiences

El Hierro's rich cultural heritage is reflected in its unique traditions, festivals, and historical sites.

8.6.1 Festivals and Events

El Hierro hosts several festivals throughout the year, celebrating local culture, music, and traditions. The Bajada de la Virgen de los Reyes, held every four years, is the island's most significant event. The festival involves a procession from the sanctuary of La Dehesa to Valverde, accompanied by traditional music, dance, and colorful costumes. Other notable festivals include the Fiesta de San Simón in October and the Fiesta de Nuestra Señora de la Candelaria in February.

8.6.2 Museums and Historical Sites

El Hierro is home to several interesting museums and historical sites that offer insights into the island's history and culture. The Ecomuseum of Guinea, located in the El Golfo Valley, features a reconstructed village that showcases traditional Herreño architecture and way of life. The Garoé Tree, an ancient holy tree that was once a vital source of water for the island's inhabitants, is another significant historical site.

8.6.3 Local Craftsmanship

El Hierro is known for its traditional craftsmanship, particularly pottery and weaving. Visitors can explore local workshops and purchase handmade souvenirs, such as ceramics, textiles, and jewelry. The village of El Pinar is a great place to learn about and experience these traditional crafts.

8.7 Adventure and Outdoor Activities

For adventure seekers, El Hierro offers a wide range of outdoor activities that take advantage of its diverse landscapes.

8.7.1 Hiking

El Hierro is a hiker's paradise, with an extensive network of trails that traverse its varied terrain. Popular trails include:

Camino de Jinama: A challenging trail that ascends from the El Golfo Valley to the highlands, offering breathtaking views and diverse landscapes.

Ruta de los Miradores: A scenic route that connects several viewpoints across the island, providing stunning panoramas of the coast, valleys, and mountains.

Sendero de la Llanía: A loop trail that passes through lush forests, volcanic craters, and picturesque villages, showcasing the island's natural beauty.

8.7.2 Diving and Snorkeling

El Hierro's clear waters and rich marine biodiversity make it a top destination for diving and snorkeling. The El Hierro Marine Reserve near La Restinga offers some of the best diving spots in Europe, with vibrant coral reefs, underwater volcanic formations, and abundant marine life. Several dive centers on the island provide courses and guided dives for all levels.

8.7.3 Paragliding

The island's dramatic landscapes and favorable weather conditions make it an ideal location for paragliding. Several companies offer tandem flights, allowing visitors to experience the thrill of soaring above El Hierro's stunning scenery.

8.8 Wellness and Relaxation

El Hierro's tranquil environment and natural beauty make it an ideal destination for wellness and relaxation. Many hotels and guesthouses offer spa services, wellness programs, and yoga retreats. The island's natural elements, such as aloe vera and volcanic stones, are often incorporated into treatments, enhancing the experience.

8.9 Family-Friendly Activities

Families will find plenty to do in El Hierro, with attractions catering to all ages. Highlights include:

Ecomuseum of Guinea: The reconstructed village provides an educational and interactive experience for children, showcasing traditional Herreño life.

Natural Swimming Pools: Charco Azul and Pozo de las Calcosas offer safe and enjoyable swimming spots for families, with calm waters and beautiful surroundings.

El Hierro Marine Reserve: Snorkeling and boat tours in the marine reserve provide an opportunity for families to explore the island's underwater world and learn about marine conservation.

8.10 Sustainable Tourism in El Hierro

El Hierro is committed to promoting sustainable tourism practices, with efforts to preserve its natural landscapes and cultural heritage. The island has implemented various initiatives to reduce its environmental impact, including the use of renewable energy sources and the promotion of eco-friendly activities. Visitors are encouraged to support local businesses, participate in conservation efforts, and minimize their environmental footprint.

Conclusion

El Hierro's rugged landscapes, pristine waters, and commitment to sustainability make it a standout destination within the Canary Islands. Whether you're seeking adventure, relaxation, or cultural immersion, El Hierro offers an unforgettable travel experience. As we continue to explore the Canary Islands in the following chapters, the diverse offerings of each island will further illuminate the remarkable appeal of this archipelago.

Chapter 9: Planning Your Trip to the Canary Islands

9.1 Introduction to Planning

Planning a trip to the Canary Islands requires some forethought to ensure you make the most of your visit. Each island offers unique experiences, and understanding the logistics, best times to visit, and key considerations will help you craft a memorable and enjoyable journey. This chapter covers essential travel planning information, including visa requirements, accommodation options, transportation, and tips for a smooth trip.

9.2 Visa and Entry Requirements

9.2.1 Visa Requirements

For most travelers, visiting the Canary Islands is straightforward. As part of Spain and the European Union, the Canary Islands follow the Schengen Agreement, which allows for visa-free travel for citizens of many countries for up to 90 days within a 180-day period. Citizens of the EU, EEA, and Switzerland do not need a visa. Travelers from the United States, Canada, Australia, and other visa-exempt countries can also visit without a visa for short stays.

9.2.2 Passport Validity

Ensure your passport is valid for at least six months beyond your intended stay. Even if your country allows entry with less validity, having six months' buffer is a good practice to avoid any issues.

9.2.3 Travel Insurance

While not mandatory, travel insurance is highly recommended. It can cover medical emergencies, trip cancellations, lost luggage, and other unforeseen events. Make sure your insurance covers activities you plan to do, such as hiking or water sports.

9.3 Best Time to Visit

9.3.1 Weather Considerations

The Canary Islands enjoy a subtropical climate, making them a year-round destination. However, the best time to visit can depend on your activities and preferences:

Summer (June to September): Ideal for beach vacations, water sports, and outdoor activities. Expect warmer temperatures and more tourists.

Winter (December to February): Perfect for escaping colder climates, with mild temperatures and fewer crowds. It's also a good time for hiking and exploring without the intense heat.

Spring (March to May) and Autumn (October to November): These shoulder seasons offer pleasant weather, blooming flora, and fewer tourists, making it an excellent time for all-around activities.

9.3.2 Festivals and Events

Consider timing your visit to coincide with local festivals for a richer cultural experience. Notable events include the Carnival of Santa Cruz de Tenerife, Fiesta de San Juan, and various island-specific celebrations.

9.4 Accommodation Options

The Canary Islands offer a wide range of accommodation options to suit all budgets and preferences.

9.4.1 Luxury Hotels and Resorts

For a luxurious stay, the islands boast several high-end hotels and resorts, particularly in Tenerife and Gran Canaria. These accommodations often feature private beaches, spas, gourmet dining, and premium services.

9.4.2 Mid-Range Hotels

Mid-range hotels and guesthouses provide comfortable lodging with good amenities. They are widely available across all the islands, offering a balance between comfort and affordability.

9.4.3 Budget Options

Budget travelers can find hostels, budget hotels, and vacation rentals offering basic amenities at affordable prices. Many budget accommodations are centrally located, providing easy access to local attractions and public transport.

9.4.4 Rural Accommodations

For a unique experience, consider staying in rural houses or "casas rurales." These accommodations, often set in picturesque countryside or traditional villages, offer a chance to experience local life and nature up close.

9.5 Transportation

9.5.1 Getting Between the Islands

Traveling between the Canary Islands is convenient, with several options available:

Flights: Binter Canarias and Canaryfly operate frequent inter-island flights. Flying is the quickest way to travel between islands, especially for longer distances.

Ferries: Naviera Armas and Fred. Olsen Express offer regular ferry services between the islands. Ferries are a scenic way to travel and often accommodate vehicles.

9.5.2 Getting Around the Islands

Each island has its transportation system to help you get around:

Public Buses: Most islands have reliable bus services covering major towns and tourist areas. TITSA operates in Tenerife, Global in Gran Canaria, and Tiadhe in Fuerteventura.

Car Rentals: Renting a car is highly recommended for exploring at your own pace, especially on islands with extensive natural attractions.

Taxis: Taxis are readily available in urban areas and can be a convenient option for shorter trips.

Bicycles and Scooters: Many islands offer bike and scooter rentals, providing an eco-friendly and fun way to explore.

9.6 Essential Packing Tips

Packing for the Canary Islands depends on the season and planned activities. Here are some essentials:

Clothing: Lightweight, breathable clothing for the day and a light jacket or sweater for cooler evenings. Comfortable walking shoes are a must for exploring and hiking.

Beach Gear: Swimwear, sunhat, sunglasses, and high-SPF sunscreen. A beach bag and flip-flops are also handy.

Hiking Gear: Sturdy hiking boots, moisture-wicking clothing, a hat, and a small backpack. Don't forget a reusable water bottle.

Travel Essentials: Travel documents, insurance information, maps or guidebooks, and any necessary medications. A universal power adapter is useful for international travelers.

9.7 Health and Safety

9.7.1 Health Precautions

The Canary Islands have a good healthcare system with hospitals and clinics available on all major islands. While there are no mandatory vaccinations for entry, it's a good idea to be up-to-date on routine vaccines. Carry any prescription medications you need and consider bringing a basic first aid kit.

9.7.2 Safety Tips

The Canary Islands are generally safe, but it's always wise to take standard precautions:

Personal Safety: Keep an eye on your belongings, especially in crowded areas. Use hotel safes for valuables.

Natural Hazards: When hiking, stay on marked trails and be aware of weather conditions. Respect the ocean's power and pay attention to beach safety flags.

Emergency Numbers: The emergency number in Spain is 112. It's useful to have local emergency contacts and the address of your accommodation handy.

9.8 Tips for a Smooth Trip

9.8.1 Language

Spanish is the official language of the Canary Islands. While many people in tourist areas speak English, learning a few basic Spanish phrases can enhance your travel experience and help you connect with locals.

9.8.2 Currency and Payments

The currency used is the Euro (€). Credit and debit cards are widely accepted, but it's a good idea to carry some cash for smaller establishments and markets. ATMs are readily available.

9.8.3 Local Etiquette

Respect local customs and traditions. Greetings often involve a handshake or cheek kisses. Dress modestly when visiting religious sites. Tipping is appreciated but not mandatory; rounding up the bill or leaving a small amount for good service is customary.

9.8.4 Internet and Connectivity

Wi-Fi is widely available in hotels, cafes, and restaurants. Consider purchasing a local SIM card or an international plan if you need continuous connectivity. Major mobile operators include Movistar, Vodafone, and Orange.

9.9 Making the Most of Your Visit

9.9.1 Explore Beyond the Tourist Spots

While popular tourist spots are worth visiting, take time to explore lesser-known areas. Small villages, local markets, and hidden trails offer a more authentic experience and a chance to connect with the local culture.

9.9.2 Try Local Cuisine

Don't miss the opportunity to sample local Canarian dishes. Each island has its specialties, from "papas arrugadas" and "mojo" sauces to fresh seafood and traditional desserts.

9.9.3 Participate in Local Activities

Engage in local activities and traditions, such as attending a festival, joining a guided hike, or learning about traditional crafts. These experiences provide deeper insights into the island's culture and lifestyle.

Conclusion

Planning a trip to the Canary Islands involves considering various factors, from entry requirements and the best time to visit to accommodation options and transportation. By preparing ahead and understanding what each island offers, you can create a travel itinerary that maximizes your experience and enjoyment. As we continue to explore the unique characteristics of each island in the following chapters, you will gain further insights into the diverse and captivating destinations within the Canary Islands.

Chapter 10: Exploring Canary Island Cuisine

10.1 Introduction to Canary Island Cuisine

The Canary Islands' cuisine is a rich tapestry woven from Spanish, African, and Latin American influences, reflecting the archipelago's history and geographic location. Known for its simplicity, freshness, and flavorful ingredients, Canarian food is a delightful experience for any visitor. This chapter explores the culinary traditions of the Canary Islands, highlighting essential dishes, drinks, and the best places to savor these local flavors.

10.2 Traditional Dishes

10.2.1 Papas Arrugadas

Papas arrugadas, or "wrinkled potatoes," are small, unpeeled potatoes boiled in heavily salted water until they form a wrinkled skin. They are typically served with mojo sauces, making them a staple of Canarian cuisine.

Mojo Rojo: A red sauce made with red peppers, garlic, cumin, olive oil, and vinegar. It is slightly spicy and pairs perfectly with the potatoes.

Mojo Verde: A green sauce made with green peppers, cilantro or parsley, garlic, cumin, olive oil, and vinegar. This sauce is milder and often accompanies fish dishes.

10.2.2 Sancocho Canario

Sancocho Canario is a traditional fish stew, usually made with salted fish (often wreckfish or grouper), potatoes, and sweet potatoes. The dish is typically served with gofio escaldado (a type of thick flour-based paste) and mojo sauces.

10.2.3 Ropa Vieja

Originally a Cuban dish, ropa vieja has been adapted in the Canary Islands. It is a flavorful stew made with shredded beef or chicken, chickpeas, potatoes, tomatoes, and various spices. This dish showcases the blending of cultures and culinary traditions within the islands.

10.2.4 Potaje de Berros

Potaje de berros is a hearty watercress soup, a traditional favorite in the Canaries. It includes ingredients such as watercress, potatoes, corn, pork, and beans, making it a nutritious and filling meal.

10.2.5 Gofio

Gofio is a type of flour made from roasted grains (typically maize or wheat) and is a dietary staple in the Canary Islands. It can be eaten in various forms, such as mixed with milk for breakfast, used as a thickener in soups and stews, or made into a doughy paste called gofio amasado.

10.3 Seafood Delights

Given the Canary Islands' location, seafood plays a significant role in the local diet. Here are some must-try seafood dishes:

10.3.1 Pescado a la Sal

Pescado a la sal is a popular dish where fresh fish is baked in a crust of coarse sea salt, which locks in moisture and enhances the flavor. The fish is typically served whole and filleted at the table.

10.3.2 Calamares a la Romana

Calamares a la romana are battered and deep-fried squid rings, often served as a tapa or appetizer. They are typically accompanied by lemon wedges and sometimes aioli (garlic mayonnaise).

10.3.3 Gambas al Ajillo

Gambas al ajillo are prawns sautéed in olive oil with garlic, chili peppers, and parsley. This dish is a favorite in tapas bars across the islands and is often enjoyed with crusty bread to soak up the flavorful oil.

10.3.4 Pulpo a la Gallega

Originally from Galicia but popular in the Canaries, pulpo a la gallega is octopus cooked and seasoned with olive oil, paprika, and sea salt. It is often served on a wooden plate with boiled potatoes.

10.4 Meat and Poultry

While seafood is prominent, the Canary Islands also offer delicious meat and poultry dishes.

10.4.1 Conejo en Salmorejo

Conejo en salmorejo is a traditional rabbit stew marinated in a sauce made from garlic, paprika, wine, vinegar, and various herbs. The marinated rabbit is then slow-cooked until tender and served with potatoes or gofio.

10.4.2 Pollo al Ajillo

Pollo al ajillo is a garlic chicken dish made by marinating chicken pieces in garlic, white wine, and herbs, then frying them until golden. This simple yet flavorful dish is a common feature at local restaurants.

10.5 Vegetarian Options

The Canary Islands offer several vegetarian-friendly dishes that highlight local produce and flavors.

10.5.1 Pimientos de Padrón

Pimientos de padrón are small green peppers fried in olive oil and sprinkled with coarse sea salt. They are typically mild, but occasionally one will be hot, adding an element of surprise to the dish.

10.5.2 Queso Asado

Queso asado is grilled or fried cheese, often served with mojo sauces. Local cheeses, such as queso de cabra (goat cheese), are used, providing a deliciously creamy texture and rich flavor.

10.5.3 Ensalada Canaria

Ensalada canaria is a refreshing salad made with local ingredients such as tomatoes, onions, boiled potatoes, and olives. It is often dressed with olive oil and vinegar and sometimes includes hard-boiled eggs or tuna.

10.6 Desserts

The Canary Islands have a variety of sweet treats that are sure to satisfy any dessert lover.

10.6.1 Bienmesabe

Bienmesabe, meaning "tastes good to me," is a rich dessert made from ground almonds, honey, sugar, and eggs. It is often served with ice cream or as a filling for cakes and pastries.

10.6.2 Frangollo

Frangollo is a traditional Canarian pudding made from cornmeal, milk, sugar, lemon zest, and raisins. It has a creamy texture and a sweet, comforting flavor.

10.6.3 Tarta de Queso

Tarta de queso is a Canarian version of cheesecake, often made with local goat cheese. It has a unique flavor and is typically served with a fruit sauce or compote.

10.7 Drinks

No culinary exploration of the Canary Islands would be complete without sampling the local beverages.

10.7.1 Wine

The Canary Islands produce excellent wines, thanks to their volcanic soil and favorable climate. Notable varieties include:

Malvasía: A sweet white wine that is one of the most famous Canarian wines.

Listán Negro: A red wine with a distinctive flavor, often grown in the unique vineyards of Lanzarote.

Vijariego: Both a red and white variety, offering rich and aromatic profiles.

10.7.2 Ron Miel

Ron miel is a traditional honey rum, a sweet liqueur made by blending rum with honey. It is often enjoyed as a digestif and is a popular souvenir for visitors.

10.7.3 Barraquito

Barraquito is a layered coffee drink typically made with espresso, condensed milk, milk, and a splash of Licor 43, a Spanish liqueur. It is often garnished with lemon zest and cinnamon.

10.8 Where to Eat

10.8.1 Guachinches

Guachinches are traditional Canarian eateries, often family-run, serving homemade dishes and local wine. They offer an authentic and affordable way to experience Canarian cuisine. These establishments are typically found in the north of Tenerife but can be spotted on other islands as well.

10.8.2 Tapas Bars

Tapas bars are ubiquitous across the Canary Islands, offering a variety of small plates that allow you to sample a wide range of flavors. Look for busy bars with locals, as they often indicate the best food.

10.8.3 Restaurants

From high-end dining to casual beachside eateries, the Canary Islands offer a diverse range of restaurants catering to all tastes and budgets. Many restaurants focus on fresh, local ingredients and traditional recipes.

Conclusion

The culinary landscape of the Canary Islands is as diverse and vibrant as the islands themselves. From traditional dishes and fresh seafood to unique desserts and local drinks, there is something to satisfy every palate. Exploring Canarian cuisine is an integral part of the travel experience, providing delicious insights into the islands' rich cultural heritage. As we continue to explore the Canary Islands in the following chapters, the diverse offerings of each island will further illuminate the remarkable appeal of this archipelago.

Chapter 11: Outdoor Activities in the Canary Islands

11.1 Introduction to Outdoor Activities

The Canary Islands, with their diverse landscapes, mild climate, and stunning natural beauty, are a paradise for outdoor enthusiasts. Whether you're a thrill-seeker looking for adventure or someone who enjoys tranquil nature walks, the archipelago offers a wide range of activities to suit all interests and fitness levels. This chapter explores the various outdoor activities available in the Canary Islands, from hiking and water sports to cycling and wildlife watching.

11.2 Hiking and Trekking

The varied terrain of the Canary Islands makes them an ideal destination for hiking and trekking. Each island offers unique trails that showcase its natural beauty and provide opportunities for exploration and adventure.

11.2.1 Tenerife

Tenerife boasts an extensive network of hiking trails, from coastal walks to challenging mountain treks.

Mount Teide: Hiking to the summit of Mount Teide, Spain's highest peak, is a challenging but rewarding experience. The trail offers stunning views of the island and beyond. The summit can be reached via a cable car, but the final ascent requires a permit.

Anaga Rural Park: Located in the northeast, Anaga Rural Park offers lush forests, dramatic cliffs, and scenic trails. Popular hikes include the Taganana to Afur trail and the Circular de Taborno.

Masca Gorge: This picturesque trail descends through a deep ravine from the village of Masca to the coast. It's a demanding hike but offers spectacular scenery.

11.2.2 Gran Canaria

Gran Canaria's diverse landscapes provide a range of hiking opportunities.

Roque Nublo: One of the island's most iconic landmarks, Roque Nublo offers a relatively easy hike with breathtaking views. The trail passes through pine forests and rocky terrain.

Barranco de Guayadeque: This ravine features lush vegetation, cave houses, and several hiking trails that vary in difficulty. The trail to Montaña de las Tierras is particularly popular.

Pico de las Nieves: The highest point on the island, Pico de las Nieves, offers panoramic views and several hiking routes that traverse the island's central mountains.

11.2.3 La Palma

Known for its lush landscapes and extensive trail network, La Palma is a hiker's paradise.

Caldera de Taburiente: This national park features numerous trails, including the popular Ruta de la Crestería, which offers stunning views of the caldera and surrounding peaks.

Ruta de los Volcanes: This trail traverses the island's volcanic ridge, offering a challenging hike with spectacular views of craters and lava fields.

Bosque de Los Tilos: A lush laurel forest with well-marked trails, including a path to the impressive Cascada de Los Tilos waterfall.

11.2.4 La Gomera

La Gomera's rugged terrain and ancient forests make it ideal for hiking.

Garajonay National Park: This UNESCO World Heritage site features ancient laurel forests and numerous trails, including the popular Alto de Garajonay hike, which offers panoramic views from the island's highest point.

Valle Gran Rey: The valley offers a range of hiking options, from coastal walks to challenging mountain trails. The route from Arure to Valle Gran Rey is particularly scenic.

Barranco de Guarimiar: A dramatic ravine with a challenging trail that offers stunning views and a glimpse into the island's geological history.

11.2.5 Fuerteventura

Fuerteventura's arid landscapes and coastal trails offer unique hiking experiences.

Betancuria Rural Park: This park features rugged terrain and several hiking routes, including the challenging Pico de la Zarza trail, which offers panoramic views from the island's highest point.

Montaña de Tindaya: Known as the Sacred Mountain, this hike provides stunning views of the island's northern region and its coastline.

Cofete Beach: The hike to Cofete Beach offers a mix of coastal and mountain scenery, ending at one of the island's most beautiful and remote beaches.

11.2.6 Lanzarote

Lanzarote's volcanic landscapes offer a unique hiking experience.

Timanfaya National Park: While hiking within the park is restricted to guided tours, the Ruta de los Volcanes trail outside the park offers a self-guided exploration of the island's volcanic terrain.

La Geria: This wine-growing region features hiking trails that wind through volcanic soil and vineyards, offering a unique cultural and natural experience.

Caldera Blanca: A moderate hike that takes you to the rim of a large volcanic crater, providing stunning views of the surrounding landscape.

11.2.7 El Hierro

El Hierro's remote and rugged terrain offers excellent hiking opportunities.

La Frontera Rural Park: This park features a mix of volcanic landscapes and lush forests, with several trails that offer breathtaking views and diverse flora and fauna.

El Sabinar: This trail leads through a unique forest of ancient, wind-sculpted juniper trees, providing a fascinating landscape for exploration.

Camino de Jinama: A challenging trail that ascends from the El Golfo Valley to the highlands, offering stunning views and diverse landscapes.

11.3 Water Sports

The Canary Islands' clear waters, consistent winds, and diverse marine life make them a paradise for water sports enthusiasts.

11.3.1 Surfing

The Canary Islands offer some of the best surfing conditions in Europe, with consistent waves and a variety of breaks suitable for all levels.

Tenerife: Playa de Las Américas and Playa del Socorro are popular surfing spots, offering a range of breaks for different skill levels.

Gran Canaria: Las Canteras and Playa del Inglés are well-known surfing beaches, with consistent waves and surf schools for beginners.

Fuerteventura: Known as the "Hawaii of Europe," Fuerteventura offers world-class surfing conditions, particularly at spots like El Cotillo and La Pared.

Lanzarote: Famara Beach and La Santa are top surfing destinations, offering powerful waves and a vibrant surf community.

11.3.2 Windsurfing and Kitesurfing

The consistent trade winds make the Canary Islands ideal for windsurfing and kitesurfing.

Tenerife: El Médano is a renowned windsurfing and kitesurfing spot, offering consistent winds and excellent facilities.

Fuerteventura: Sotavento Beach is a world-famous windsurfing and kitesurfing destination, hosting international competitions and offering ideal conditions for all skill levels.

Gran Canaria: Pozo Izquierdo is a popular windsurfing spot, known for its strong winds and challenging conditions.

11.3.3 Scuba Diving and Snorkeling

The Canary Islands' clear waters and diverse marine life make them a top destination for diving and snorkeling.

El Hierro: La Restinga Marine Reserve offers some of the best diving in Europe, with vibrant coral reefs, underwater volcanic formations, and abundant marine life.

Lanzarote: The Museo Atlántico, an underwater museum featuring sculptures by Jason deCaires Taylor, is a unique diving experience. The island also offers excellent diving spots at Playa Chica and Puerto del Carmen.

Gran Canaria: The wreck of the Arona and the El Cabrón Marine Reserve are popular diving sites, offering diverse marine life and underwater landscapes.

Tenerife: The island offers numerous diving spots, including Los Cristianos and Los Gigantes, known for their clear waters and diverse marine ecosystems.

11.3.4 Kayaking and Stand-Up Paddleboarding (SUP)

The calm coastal waters of the Canary Islands are perfect for kayaking and stand-up paddleboarding.

Tenerife: Los Gigantes offers stunning coastal cliffs and sea caves to explore by kayak or SUP.

Gran Canaria: The southern coast, particularly around Puerto de Mogán, provides calm waters and beautiful scenery for paddling.

La Palma: The island's rugged coastline offers secluded coves and pristine waters for kayaking and SUP.

11.4 Cycling

The diverse terrain and mild climate of the Canary Islands make them an excellent destination for cycling enthusiasts.

11.4.1 Road Cycling

The islands offer scenic routes with varying levels of difficulty, from coastal roads to challenging mountain climbs.

Tenerife: The route to Mount Teide is a challenging climb but offers breathtaking views. The coastal road from Santa Cruz to Los Cristianos is also popular among cyclists.

Gran Canaria: The GC-200 road from Agaete to La Aldea de San Nicolás is a stunning coastal route, while the climb to Pico de las Nieves offers a rewarding challenge.

Lanzarote: The island's quiet roads and volcanic landscapes provide excellent cycling conditions. The route from Arrecife to Timanfaya National Park is a favorite.

11.4.2 Mountain Biking

The islands' rugged terrain offers exciting opportunities for mountain biking.

Tenerife: The Anaga and Teno mountain ranges offer challenging trails with stunning views. The route through Teide National Park is also popular among mountain bikers.

Gran Canaria: The island's central mountains provide numerous trails, including the popular route from Ayacata to Cruz de Tejeda.

La Palma: The island's lush forests and volcanic landscapes offer excellent mountain biking conditions. The route from El Pilar to Fuencaliente is a favorite among cyclists.

11.5 Wildlife Watching

The Canary Islands' diverse ecosystems provide excellent opportunities for wildlife watching.

11.5.1 Birdwatching

The islands are home to several endemic bird species and serve as a stopover for migratory birds.

La Gomera: The Garajonay National Park is a prime location for spotting endemic species such as the La Palma chaffinch and the Bolle's pigeon.

Tenerife: The Anaga Rural Park and Teide National Park offer opportunities to see the blue chaffinch and the Canary Islands chiffchaff.

Fuerteventura: The island's arid landscapes provide a habitat for the houbara bustard and the Egyptian vulture.

11.5.2 Whale and Dolphin Watching

The waters around the Canary Islands are home to several species of whales and dolphins, making it a prime destination for marine mammal watching.

Tenerife: The waters between Tenerife and La Gomera are one of the best spots for whale and dolphin watching, with frequent sightings of pilot whales and bottlenose dolphins.

Gran Canaria: Whale watching tours from Puerto Rico offer opportunities to see various species, including sperm whales and common dolphins.

La Palma: The island's clear waters provide excellent conditions for marine mammal watching, with tours departing from Santa Cruz de La Palma.

11.6 Rock Climbing and Caving

The volcanic landscapes of the Canary Islands offer unique rock climbing and caving opportunities.

11.6.1 Rock Climbing

The islands' rugged terrain provides a range of climbing routes for all levels.

Gran Canaria: The island's central mountains, particularly around Roque Nublo, offer numerous climbing routes with stunning views.

Tenerife: The Teno and Anaga mountain ranges provide excellent climbing conditions, with routes suitable for both beginners and experienced climbers.

Lanzarote: The island's volcanic cliffs offer unique climbing opportunities, particularly in the Timanfaya National Park area.

11.6.2 Caving

The islands' volcanic origins have created a network of caves and lava tubes, offering exciting caving experiences.

Tenerife: The Cueva del Viento, one of the longest lava tubes in the world, offers guided tours that explore its unique geological formations.

Lanzarote: The Cueva de los Verdes and Jameos del Agua are part of a large lava tube system, offering guided tours that highlight the island's volcanic history.

La Palma: The island's volcanic terrain provides several caving opportunities, particularly in the southern region near the San Antonio Volcano.

Conclusion

The Canary Islands offer a diverse range of outdoor activities that cater to all interests and fitness levels. From hiking and water sports to cycling and wildlife watching, the archipelago's unique landscapes and favorable climate provide endless opportunities for adventure and exploration. As we continue to delve into the unique characteristics of each island in the following chapters, you will gain further insights into the remarkable outdoor experiences that make the Canary Islands a premier destination for nature lovers and adventure enthusiasts.

Chapter 12: Cultural and Historical Exploration in the Canary Islands

12.1 Introduction to Cultural and Historical Exploration

The Canary Islands are not only known for their stunning natural landscapes but also for their rich cultural heritage and historical significance. From ancient indigenous traditions to colonial history and vibrant modern-day festivals, the archipelago offers a diverse cultural tapestry for visitors to explore. This chapter delves into the cultural and historical attractions of the Canary Islands, highlighting key sites, traditions, and events that provide a deeper understanding of the islands' unique identity.

12.2 Indigenous Heritage

The Canary Islands were originally inhabited by indigenous people known as the Guanches (in Tenerife and La Gomera) and other tribes on different islands. Their legacy is still evident in various archaeological sites, artifacts, and cultural practices.

12.2.1 Archaeological Sites

Cueva Pintada (Gran Canaria): This archaeological park and museum in Gáldar features well-preserved cave paintings and offers insights into the life and culture of the ancient Canarians.

Cueva de los Verdes (Lanzarote): Part of a larger lava tube system, this cave was used by indigenous people and later by locals seeking refuge from pirate attacks.

El Julan (El Hierro): This site features ancient petroglyphs created by the Bimbache people. The visitor center provides information on the island's pre-Hispanic history.

12.2.2 Museums

Museum of Nature and Archaeology (Tenerife): Located in Santa Cruz de Tenerife, this museum houses an extensive collection of artifacts related to the indigenous Guanche culture, including mummies, tools, and pottery.

Archaeological Museum of La Gomera: Situated in San Sebastián de La Gomera, this museum offers exhibits on the island's pre-Hispanic history and the Guanche people.

Museo Canario (Gran Canaria): Located in Las Palmas, this museum features a comprehensive collection of artifacts from the island's indigenous inhabitants.

12.3 Colonial History

The Canary Islands played a significant role in the age of exploration and colonial expansion. The islands served as a stopover for explorers, including Christopher Columbus, on their way to the New World.

12.3.1 Historic Sites

Casa de Colón (Gran Canaria): This museum in Las Palmas is dedicated to Christopher Columbus and his voyages. The building itself is a beautiful example of colonial architecture.

Torre del Conde (La Gomera): A medieval fortress in San Sebastián de La Gomera, built in the 15th century to protect against pirate attacks. It is one of the island's oldest structures.

San Cristóbal de La Laguna (Tenerife): A UNESCO World Heritage site, this historic town features well-preserved colonial architecture, cobbled streets, and significant religious buildings, such as the Cathedral of San Cristóbal de La Laguna.

12.3.2 Churches and Religious Sites

Cathedral of Santa Ana (Gran Canaria): Located in the Vegueta district of Las Palmas, this cathedral is a stunning example of Gothic and Neoclassical architecture. It is one of the most important religious buildings in the Canary Islands.

Church of the Conception (Tenerife): Situated in San Cristóbal de La Laguna, this church is one of the oldest on the island and features beautiful Mudejar-style architecture.

Basilica of Our Lady of Candelaria (Tenerife): A major pilgrimage site, this basilica is dedicated to the Virgin of Candelaria, the patron saint of the Canary Islands.

12.4 Festivals and Traditions

The Canary Islands are renowned for their vibrant festivals, which celebrate everything from religious events to local culture and history.

12.4.1 Carnival

The Carnival of Santa Cruz de Tenerife is one of the largest and most spectacular carnivals in the world. It features elaborate costumes, parades, music, and dancing, attracting visitors from around the globe. Other islands also celebrate carnival with their own unique flair.

12.4.2 Fiesta de San Juan

Celebrated on June 24th, the Fiesta de San Juan marks the summer solstice with bonfires, fireworks, and various festivities. Each island has its own way of celebrating, but common activities include jumping over bonfires and bathing in the sea at midnight.

12.4.3 Bajada de la Virgen de los Reyes

Held every four years on El Hierro, this pilgrimage honors the island's patron saint, the Virgin of Los Reyes. The event involves a procession from the sanctuary of La Dehesa to the capital, Valverde, accompanied by traditional music and dance.

12.4.4 Día de Canarias

Celebrated on May 30th, Día de Canarias commemorates the anniversary of the autonomous Canary Islands' first session in 1983. Festivities include traditional music, dance, sports, and culinary events, showcasing the rich cultural heritage of the islands.

12.5 Local Crafts and Markets

The Canary Islands are known for their traditional crafts, which reflect the islands' history and cultural influences. Visiting local markets and workshops provides an opportunity to see artisans at work and purchase unique souvenirs.

12.5.1 Pottery

Traditional Canarian pottery is often made without a potter's wheel, a technique passed down from the indigenous Guanche people. The village of La Atalaya in Gran Canaria is famous for its pottery workshops.

12.5.2 Basketry

Basket weaving is a common craft across the islands, using materials such as palm leaves, reed, and willow. The baskets are used for various purposes, from carrying goods to decorative items.

12.5.3 Embroidery and Lace

The islands, particularly La Palma and Tenerife, are known for their intricate embroidery and lacework. These traditional crafts are often seen in tablecloths, clothing, and accessories.

12.5.4 Markets

Mercado de Vegueta (Gran Canaria): This historic market in Las Palmas offers a wide range of local produce, crafts, and souvenirs.

Mercado Nuestra Señora de África (Tenerife): Located in Santa Cruz de Tenerife, this market is a great place to find fresh produce, local delicacies, and handmade crafts.

Agulo Market (La Gomera): A small market held in the picturesque village of Agulo, offering local crafts, food, and souvenirs.

12.6 Music and Dance

Music and dance are integral parts of Canarian culture, with traditional folk music and dance styles that reflect the islands' diverse influences.

12.6.1 Folklore Music

Traditional Canarian music is characterized by the use of string instruments such as the timple (a small guitar-like instrument), guitar, and bandurria. Popular music styles include:

Isa: A lively folk dance often performed at festivals and celebrations.

Folia: A slower, more melancholic style of music and dance.

Malagueñas: A type of folk music with influences from Andalusia.

12.6.2 Traditional Dance

Traditional Canarian dance is often performed at festivals and celebrations, featuring colorful costumes and intricate choreography. The dances often tell stories of daily life, love, and historical events.

12.6.3 Modern Music and Festivals

The Canary Islands also have a vibrant contemporary music scene, with numerous music festivals held throughout the year, showcasing genres such as jazz, rock, and electronic music.

Canary Islands Music Festival: An annual classical music festival held in various venues across the islands, featuring performances by renowned international and local artists.

Festival Internacional de Jazz de Canarias: A popular jazz festival that attracts musicians from around the world to perform in stunning outdoor settings.

Conclusion

The Canary Islands offer a rich cultural and historical tapestry that adds depth to any visit. From ancient indigenous heritage and colonial history to vibrant festivals and traditional crafts, there is much to explore and appreciate. By delving into the cultural and historical aspects of the islands, visitors can gain a deeper understanding of the unique identity and charm of this remarkable archipelago. As we continue to explore the Canary Islands in the following chapters, the diverse offerings of each island will further illuminate the remarkable appeal of this destination.

Chapter 13: Family-Friendly Activities in the Canary Islands

13.1 Introduction to Family-Friendly Activities

The Canary Islands are an excellent destination for family vacations, offering a variety of activities and attractions that cater to all ages. From interactive museums and animal parks to outdoor adventures and beach fun, the archipelago provides endless opportunities for memorable family experiences. This chapter explores the best family-friendly activities across the Canary Islands, ensuring that every member of the family can enjoy a fantastic holiday.

13.2 Amusement and Theme Parks

13.2.1 Siam Park (Tenerife)

Siam Park is one of the largest and most popular water parks in Europe, located in Costa Adeje, Tenerife. The park features a Thai theme and offers a wide range of attractions, including:

The Dragon: A thrilling water slide that simulates zero gravity.

Siam Beach: A man-made beach with the world's largest artificial waves.

The Lost City: A water playground designed specifically for children, with shallow pools and smaller slides.

13.2.2 Loro Parque (Tenerife)

Loro Parque is a world-renowned animal park located in Puerto de la Cruz, Tenerife. The park is home to a diverse collection of animals, including parrots, dolphins, orcas, and gorillas. Highlights include:

Penguinarium: One of the world's largest indoor penguin exhibitions.

Orca Ocean: A spectacular show featuring orcas.

Planet Penguin: A state-of-the-art penguin habitat.

13.2.3 Aqualand Maspalomas (Gran Canaria)

Aqualand Maspalomas is a large water park in Gran Canaria, offering a variety of water slides, wave pools, and attractions for all ages. Popular features include:

Kamikaze: A high-speed water slide for thrill-seekers.

Pirate's Cove: A water playground with slides and splash zones for younger children.

Lazy River: A relaxing float along a winding river.

13.2.4 Rancho Texas Lanzarote Park (Lanzarote)

Rancho Texas Lanzarote Park is an animal and water park located near Puerto del Carmen, Lanzarote. The park offers a range of activities, including:

Animal Shows: Featuring birds of prey, sea lions, and parrots.

Splash Zone: A water playground with slides and pools.

Gold Mining: An interactive experience where kids can pan for "gold."

13.3 Interactive Museums and Educational Centers

13.3.1 Museo Elder de la Ciencia y la Tecnología (Gran Canaria)

The Elder Museum of Science and Technology in Las Palmas, Gran Canaria, offers interactive exhibits and hands-on activities that make learning fun for kids and adults alike. Highlights include:

Planetarium: A dome theater offering shows about the universe.

Robotics Area: Interactive exhibits showcasing the latest in robotics technology.

Science Workshops: Hands-on activities and experiments for children.

13.3.2 Museo de la Ciencia y el Cosmos (Tenerife)

The Museum of Science and the Cosmos in La Laguna, Tenerife, features interactive exhibits and educational displays that explore various scientific concepts. Highlights include:

Explora Room: An interactive space where kids can conduct experiments and learn through play.

Planetarium: Shows and presentations about space and astronomy.

Temporary Exhibits: Rotating displays on topics such as physics, biology, and technology.

13.3.3 Casa de los Balcones (Tenerife)

Located in La Orotava, Tenerife, the Casa de los Balcones is a historic house museum that offers a glimpse into traditional Canarian life. The museum features:

Traditional Crafts: Demonstrations of Canarian embroidery and lace-making.

Historic Architecture: Beautifully preserved wooden balconies and interior courtyards.

Interactive Exhibits: Hands-on activities for children, such as dressing in traditional costumes.

13.4 Outdoor Adventures

13.4.1 Camel Rides (Various Islands)

Camel rides are a popular activity in the Canary Islands, offering a unique way to explore the landscapes. Locations include:

Dunas de Maspalomas (Gran Canaria): Ride camels through the stunning sand dunes of Maspalomas.

Timanfaya National Park (Lanzarote): Experience a camel ride through the volcanic landscapes of the park.

13.4.2 Whale and Dolphin Watching (Various Islands)

The waters around the Canary Islands are home to several species of whales and dolphins. Family-friendly boat tours offer the chance to see these magnificent creatures up close. Popular departure points include:

Los Cristianos (Tenerife): Tours often spot pilot whales and bottlenose dolphins.

Puerto Rico (Gran Canaria): Regular sightings of various dolphin species and occasional whales.

La Palma: Known for its clear waters and frequent dolphin sightings.

13.4.3 Hiking and Nature Walks (Various Islands)

Many of the islands offer family-friendly hiking trails and nature walks that showcase their natural beauty.

Garajonay National Park (La Gomera): The park offers several easy trails suitable for families, including the Bosque del Cedro walk.

Anaga Rural Park (Tenerife): Family-friendly trails such as the Path of the Senses offer short, accessible hikes through lush forests.

Caldera de Taburiente National Park (La Palma): The park features various trails, including the easy walk to the Cascada de los Colores waterfall.

13.5 Beaches and Water Activities

The Canary Islands are renowned for their beautiful beaches and clear waters, providing endless opportunities for family fun.

13.5.1 Playa de Las Teresitas (Tenerife)

Playa de Las Teresitas is a man-made beach near Santa Cruz de Tenerife, featuring golden sand imported from the Sahara Desert. The calm waters and excellent facilities make it ideal for families.

13.5.2 Playa del Inglés (Gran Canaria)

Playa del Inglés is one of the most popular beaches in Gran Canaria, offering a wide range of water sports and beach activities. The beach is well-equipped with amenities, including sun loungers, parasols, and restaurants.

13.5.3 Playa de Papagayo (Lanzarote)

Playa de Papagayo is a series of pristine beaches located in the Los Ajaches Natural Park. The calm, clear waters are perfect for swimming and snorkeling, making it a great spot for families.

13.5.4 Playa de Sotavento (Fuerteventura)

Playa de Sotavento is known for its shallow lagoons and gentle waves, making it ideal for young children. The beach also offers windsurfing and kitesurfing schools for older kids and adults.

13.6 Animal Parks and Zoos

13.6.1 Palmitos Park (Gran Canaria)

Palmitos Park is a botanical garden and zoo located in the south of Gran Canaria. The park features a wide variety of animals, including birds, reptiles, and mammals. Highlights include:

Dolphinarium: Home to several dolphins, with daily shows and interactive experiences.

Bird Shows: Featuring exotic birds such as parrots and birds of prey.

Orchid House: A beautiful collection of orchids and other tropical plants.

13.6.2 Oasis Park (Fuerteventura)

Oasis Park is a large zoo and botanical garden located in La Lajita, Fuerteventura. The park offers a range of attractions, including:

Animal Shows: Featuring sea lions, birds of prey, and parrots.

Safari Experience: A guided tour through the park's savanna area, home to giraffes, zebras, and other African animals.

Camel Rides: A unique way to explore the park's landscape.

13.6.3 Jungle Park (Tenerife)

Jungle Park is a zoo and adventure park located in Arona, Tenerife. The park features a variety of animals, as well as adventure attractions such as:

Bird of Prey Show: Featuring eagles, hawks, and vultures.

Penguin Exhibit: A state-of-the-art habitat for penguins.

Bob Jungle: A toboggan run through the park's lush landscape.

13.7 Interactive Farms and Botanical Gardens

13.7.1 Finca Canarias Aloe Vera (Various Islands)

Finca Canarias Aloe Vera offers guided tours of aloe vera plantations across several islands, including Tenerife, Gran Canaria, and Lanzarote. Visitors can learn about the cultivation and processing of aloe vera and sample various aloe vera products.

13.7.2 Cactus Garden (Lanzarote)

The Cactus Garden in Guatiza, Lanzarote, is a beautifully landscaped garden featuring over 1,000 species of cacti. Designed by

César Manrique, the garden offers a unique and educational experience for families.

13.7.3 La Granja Verde (Gran Canaria)

La Granja Verde is an interactive farm located in the north of Gran Canaria. The farm offers a range of activities, including:

Animal Encounters: Meet and feed various farm animals, including goats, pigs, and chickens.

Workshops: Learn about traditional farming practices and participate in activities such as cheese-making and bread-baking.

Nature Walks: Explore the farm's gardens and orchards.

13.8 Adventure Parks and Zip Lines

13.8.1 Forestal Park (Tenerife)

Forestal Park is an adventure park located in Las Lagunetas, Tenerife. The park offers a range of activities, including:

Zip Lines: A series of thrilling zip lines through the forest.

Rope Courses: Various courses of differing difficulty levels, suitable for both children and adults.

Climbing Walls: Indoor and outdoor climbing walls for all ages.

13.8.2 GrancAventura (Gran Canaria)

GrancAventura is an adventure park located in Arucas, Gran Canaria. The park features a variety of activities, including:

Zip Lines: Multiple zip lines that offer exciting rides through the park.

Obstacle Courses: A range of courses designed for different age groups and skill levels.

Archery: An archery range where visitors can learn and practice archery skills.

13.9 Family-Friendly Festivals and Events

13.9.1 Carnival (Various Islands)

The Carnival is a major event across the Canary Islands, with colorful parades, music, and dance. Family-friendly activities include:

Children's Parades: Special parades and events designed for children.

Costume Contests: Fun contests where kids can show off their costumes.

Family Zones: Areas with games, rides, and entertainment for children.

13.9.2 Fiestas de San Juan (Various Islands)

The Fiestas de San Juan are celebrated across the Canary Islands, marking the summer solstice. Family-friendly activities include:

Bonfires: Beach bonfires and fireworks.

Nighttime Swims: Traditional midnight swims in the ocean.

Live Music and Dancing: Festivities often include live music and dance performances.

13.9.3 Día de Canarias (Various Islands)

Día de Canarias is celebrated on May 30th and includes a variety of family-friendly events, such as:

Traditional Music and Dance: Performances showcasing Canarian folk music and dance.

Cultural Workshops: Activities where children can learn about Canarian crafts and traditions.

Food Stalls: Sample local dishes and sweets.

Conclusion

The Canary Islands offer a wealth of family-friendly activities that cater to all ages and interests. From amusement parks and interactive museums to outdoor adventures and cultural festivals, there is something for every member of the family to enjoy. By exploring the diverse attractions and activities across the islands, families can create lasting memories and experience the unique charm and hospitality of the Canary Islands. As we continue to explore the archipelago in the following chapters, the diverse offerings of each island will further illuminate the remarkable appeal of this destination.

Chapter 14: Shopping and Souvenirs in the Canary Islands

14.1 Introduction to Shopping in the Canary Islands

The Canary Islands offer a unique shopping experience, combining traditional markets with modern shopping centers. Visitors can find a wide variety of products, from local crafts and delicacies to international brands and luxury items. This chapter explores the best shopping destinations across the Canary Islands, highlighting local markets, specialty shops, and shopping malls, as well as popular souvenirs to bring home.

14.2 Traditional Markets

14.2.1 Mercado de Vegueta (Gran Canaria)

Located in the historic district of Las Palmas, the Mercado de Vegueta is a vibrant market offering fresh produce, local delicacies, and handmade crafts. Highlights include:

Fresh Produce: Seasonal fruits, vegetables, and herbs.

Local Delicacies: Cheeses, cured meats, and Canarian wines.

Handmade Crafts: Pottery, textiles, and jewelry.

14.2.2 Mercado Nuestra Señora de África (Tenerife)

Situated in Santa Cruz de Tenerife, the Mercado Nuestra Señora de África is a bustling market known for its wide selection of goods. Highlights include:

Fresh Seafood: Daily catches from local fishermen.

Flowers and Plants: A colorful array of local and exotic flowers.

Traditional Foods: Gofio, mojo sauces, and tropical fruits.

14.2.3 Agulo Market (La Gomera)

The Agulo Market is held in the picturesque village of Agulo and offers a range of local products. Highlights include:

Local Produce: Fresh fruits, vegetables, and herbs.

Artisan Goods: Handmade pottery, baskets, and lacework.

Local Delicacies: Palm honey, cheeses, and baked goods.

14.3 Specialty Shops and Boutiques

14.3.1 La Molina Artesanía (Various Islands)

La Molina Artesanía is a chain of stores specializing in traditional Canarian crafts. Items include:

Pottery: Handcrafted pieces made using traditional techniques.

Textiles: Embroidered tablecloths, lace, and clothing.

Jewelry: Unique pieces inspired by Canarian culture.

14.3.2 Bodegas Monje (Tenerife)

Located in the wine-growing region of El Sauzal, Bodegas Monje offers a selection of locally produced wines. Visitors can enjoy:

Wine Tastings: Sample a variety of red, white, and rosé wines.

Wine Tours: Guided tours of the vineyard and winery.

Gourmet Products: Local cheeses, olive oil, and honey.

14.3.3 Aloe Vera Shops (Various Islands)

Aloe vera is a popular product in the Canary Islands, known for its health and beauty benefits. Specialized shops offer:

Skincare Products: Lotions, creams, and gels made from pure aloe vera.

Health Products: Aloe vera juices and supplements.

Cosmetics: Natural cosmetics incorporating aloe vera.

14.4 Shopping Centers and Malls

14.4.1 Siam Mall (Tenerife)

Siam Mall is a large shopping center located near Costa Adeje, offering a variety of stores and dining options. Highlights include:

Fashion Brands: International and Spanish fashion brands.

Electronics: Shops selling the latest gadgets and technology.

Dining Options: Restaurants, cafes, and food courts.

14.4.2 El Corte Inglés (Gran Canaria and Tenerife)

El Corte Inglés is Spain's largest department store chain, with locations in Las Palmas (Gran Canaria) and Santa Cruz (Tenerife). The store offers:

Fashion and Accessories: Designer clothing, shoes, and accessories.

Home Goods: Furniture, decor, and kitchenware.

Beauty and Cosmetics: High-end beauty products and fragrances.

14.4.3 Centro Comercial Meridiano (Tenerife)

Located in Santa Cruz de Tenerife, Centro Comercial Meridiano is a modern shopping center featuring:

Retail Stores: Fashion, electronics, and home goods.

Entertainment: A cinema, bowling alley, and arcade.

Dining: A variety of restaurants and cafes.

14.5 Popular Souvenirs

14.5.1 Gofio

Gofio is a traditional Canarian flour made from roasted grains, often used in local dishes. It makes for a unique and authentic souvenir.

14.5.2 Mojo Sauces

Mojo sauces, both red (mojo rojo) and green (mojo verde), are staple condiments in Canarian cuisine. They are available in jars, making them easy to take home.

14.5.3 Canarian Wines

The Canary Islands produce a variety of wines, including the famous Malvasía. A bottle of local wine makes a great gift or personal keepsake.

14.5.4 Pottery and Ceramics

Handcrafted pottery and ceramics, often featuring traditional designs, are popular souvenirs. Look for items such as vases, bowls, and decorative tiles.

14.5.5 Embroidery and Lace

Intricately embroidered textiles and lacework are a hallmark of Canarian craftsmanship. Tablecloths, napkins, and clothing items are beautiful and practical souvenirs.

14.5.6 Aloe Vera Products

Aloe vera products, including skincare items, health supplements, and cosmetics, are widely available and make for thoughtful gifts.

14.5.7 Palm Honey

Palm honey is a unique Canarian product made from the sap of palm trees. It has a rich, sweet flavor and is often used in desserts and as a topping for pancakes.

14.6 Tips for Shopping in the Canary Islands

14.6.1 Bargaining

While bargaining is not common in larger stores and shopping centers, it may be acceptable in local markets. Always be polite and respectful when negotiating prices.

14.6.2 Tax-Free Shopping

Non-EU residents can take advantage of tax-free shopping in the Canary Islands. Look for stores displaying the "Tax-Free" logo and remember to keep your receipts and ask for a tax-free form.

14.6.3 Supporting Local Artisans

Purchasing from local artisans and markets not only provides unique souvenirs but also supports the local economy and helps preserve traditional crafts.

14.6.4 Checking for Authenticity

When buying high-value items such as jewelry or branded goods, ensure you purchase from reputable stores to avoid counterfeit products. Ask for certificates of authenticity when applicable.

Conclusion

Shopping in the Canary Islands offers a delightful mix of traditional markets, specialty shops, and modern shopping centers. Whether you're looking for unique local crafts, delicious delicacies, or international brands, the islands have something for everyone. Bringing home a piece of the Canary Islands through souvenirs and gifts allows you to cherish your memories and share the island's charm with others. As we continue to explore the archipelago in the following chapters, the diverse offerings of each island will further illuminate the remarkable appeal of this destination.

Chapter 15: Sustainable Tourism in the Canary Islands

15.1 Introduction to Sustainable Tourism

Sustainable tourism aims to minimize the negative impacts of travel on the environment, economy, and society while maximizing the benefits. The Canary Islands, with their unique ecosystems and rich cultural heritage, are committed to promoting sustainable tourism practices. This chapter explores the efforts being made to protect the natural and cultural resources of the archipelago and provides tips for travelers on how to enjoy their visit responsibly.

15.2 Environmental Conservation

15.2.1 Protected Areas

The Canary Islands are home to numerous protected areas, including national parks, natural parks, and biosphere reserves, which help preserve the islands' unique flora and fauna.

15.2.1.1 Teide National Park (Tenerife)

Teide National Park is a UNESCO World Heritage site and home to Mount Teide, Spain's highest peak. The park's unique volcanic landscape and diverse ecosystems are protected, and visitors are encouraged to explore responsibly.

15.2.1.2 Timanfaya National Park (Lanzarote)

Timanfaya National Park features a stunning volcanic landscape formed by eruptions in the 18th century. The park's geothermal activity and unique geology are protected, with guided tours available to minimize environmental impact.

15.2.1.3 Garajonay National Park (La Gomera)

Garajonay National Park is a UNESCO World Heritage site known for its ancient laurel forests. The park's lush greenery and rich biodiversity are protected, and visitors can explore well-marked trails to minimize disturbance to the environment.

15.2.2 Marine Reserves

The Canary Islands' marine reserves protect the rich biodiversity of the surrounding waters, ensuring the sustainability of marine life and habitats.

15.2.2.1 El Hierro Marine Reserve

The El Hierro Marine Reserve near La Restinga is renowned for its clear waters and diverse marine life, making it a popular destination for divers. Strict regulations help preserve the underwater ecosystem.

15.2.2.2 La Graciosa Marine Reserve (Lanzarote)

La Graciosa Marine Reserve protects the waters around the island of La Graciosa and the northern coast of Lanzarote. The reserve supports a variety of marine species and promotes sustainable fishing practices.

15.2.3 Renewable Energy

The Canary Islands are pioneers in the use of renewable energy, with projects aimed at reducing carbon emissions and promoting sustainability.

15.2.3.1 Gorona del Viento (El Hierro)

Gorona del Viento is a hydro-wind power plant on El Hierro that aims to make the island fully self-sufficient in renewable energy. The plant combines wind turbines and pumped-storage hydroelectricity to generate clean energy.

15.2.3.2 Wind Farms (Various Islands)

Several wind farms across the Canary Islands harness the power of the trade winds to generate renewable energy, reducing reliance on fossil fuels and lowering carbon emissions.

15.3 Cultural Heritage Preservation

15.3.1 Traditional Crafts

Preserving traditional crafts is essential for maintaining the cultural heritage of the Canary Islands. Supporting local artisans helps keep these traditions alive.

15.3.1.1 Pottery

Handcrafted pottery, often made using ancient techniques, is a significant part of Canarian culture. Workshops and markets offer visitors the chance to purchase authentic pottery and support local craftsmen.

15.3.1.2 Embroidery and Lace

Intricate embroidery and lacework are traditional crafts in the Canary Islands. Purchasing these handmade items supports local artisans and helps preserve these skills for future generations.

15.3.2 Historic Sites and Museums

Visiting historic sites and museums not only provides insight into the islands' rich history but also supports their preservation.

15.3.2.1 San Cristóbal de La Laguna (Tenerife)

San Cristóbal de La Laguna is a UNESCO World Heritage site known for its well-preserved colonial architecture. Walking tours and visits to historic buildings help fund the conservation of this culturally significant town.

15.3.2.2 Casa de Colón (Gran Canaria)

The Casa de Colón museum in Las Palmas is dedicated to Christopher Columbus and his voyages. Visiting the museum supports the preservation of this historic site and its collections.

15.4 Sustainable Accommodation

15.4.1 Eco-Friendly Hotels and Resorts

Many hotels and resorts in the Canary Islands are committed to sustainable practices, such as energy conservation, waste reduction, and water management.

15.4.1.1 Hotel Hacienda del Conde (Tenerife)

Hotel Hacienda del Conde is an eco-friendly hotel that integrates sustainable practices into its operations, including solar energy, water-saving measures, and locally sourced food.

15.4.1.2 Finca de Arrieta (Lanzarote)

Finca de Arrieta is a sustainable holiday village that uses renewable energy, recycles water, and promotes eco-friendly tourism. The accommodation includes eco-lodges and yurts built with sustainable materials.

15.4.2 Rural Tourism

Staying in rural accommodations, such as "casas rurales," supports local communities and provides an authentic experience of Canarian life.

15.4.2.1 Casa Rural La Asomada del Gato (La Gomera)

Casa Rural La Asomada del Gato is a traditional rural house that offers comfortable accommodation while preserving the local architecture and supporting the rural economy.

15.4.2.2 Casa Rural La Jarita (El Hierro)

Casa Rural La Jarita is a charming rural house that promotes sustainable tourism by using eco-friendly practices and offering guests a chance to experience the island's natural beauty and traditional lifestyle.

15.5 Sustainable Travel Tips

15.5.1 Reduce, Reuse, Recycle

Bring Reusable Items: Use reusable water bottles, shopping bags, and containers to minimize waste.

Recycle: Follow local recycling guidelines to ensure waste is properly sorted and recycled.

Reduce Waste: Avoid single-use plastics and unnecessary packaging.

15.5.2 Conserve Water and Energy

Water Conservation: Take shorter showers, turn off taps when not in use, and use water-saving features in accommodations.

Energy Conservation: Turn off lights, air conditioning, and electronics when not needed. Choose energy-efficient transportation options, such as public transport, cycling, or walking.

15.5.3 Support Local Businesses

Eat Local: Choose restaurants that use locally sourced ingredients to support local farmers and reduce the carbon footprint of food transportation.

Shop Local: Purchase souvenirs and products from local artisans and markets to support the local economy and preserve cultural heritage.

Use Local Guides: Hire local guides for tours and activities to ensure your money supports the community and you gain authentic insights into the islands' culture and environment.

15.5.4 Respect Nature and Wildlife

Stay on Trails: Stick to marked trails when hiking to avoid damaging fragile ecosystems.

Don't Disturb Wildlife: Observe animals from a distance and do not feed or touch them. Follow guidelines for responsible wildlife watching.

Leave No Trace: Carry out all trash, avoid picking plants or disturbing natural features, and leave places as you found them.

15.6 Eco-Friendly Activities

15.6.1 Hiking and Nature Walks

Exploring the Canary Islands on foot is a low-impact way to enjoy their natural beauty. Choose well-maintained trails and follow sustainable hiking practices.

15.6.2 Cycling

Cycling is an eco-friendly way to explore the islands while reducing your carbon footprint. Many islands offer bike rentals and well-marked cycling routes.

15.6.3 Snorkeling and Diving

Participating in responsible snorkeling and diving practices helps protect marine ecosystems. Choose eco-friendly tour operators and follow guidelines for minimizing your impact on underwater habitats.

15.6.4 Volunteering

Volunteering with local conservation projects is a great way to give back to the community and support environmental initiatives. Opportunities include beach cleanups, wildlife monitoring, and habitat restoration.

Conclusion

The Canary Islands are committed to promoting sustainable tourism practices that protect their unique environments and cultural heritage. By making conscious choices and supporting eco-friendly initiatives, travelers can enjoy a responsible and enriching experience while helping to preserve the islands for future generations. As we continue to explore the Canary Islands in the following chapters, the diverse offerings of each island will further illuminate the remarkable appeal of this destination.

Chapter 16: Adventure Activities in the Canary Islands

16.1 Introduction to Adventure Activities

The Canary Islands are a playground for adventure enthusiasts, offering a wide range of exhilarating activities that take full advantage of the archipelago's diverse landscapes and favorable climate. From scaling volcanic peaks to exploring underwater worlds, the Canary Islands provide endless opportunities for thrill-seekers and nature lovers alike. This chapter explores some of the most exciting adventure activities available across the islands, ensuring you can plan an action-packed and unforgettable vacation.

16.2 Hiking and Trekking

16.2.1 Mount Teide Ascent (Tenerife)

Scaling Mount Teide, Spain's highest peak at 3,718 meters, is a bucket-list adventure for many hikers. The ascent can be done via several routes, with the most popular being the Montaña Blanca trail. A cable car takes you close to the summit, but the final section requires a special permit.

16.2.2 Ruta de los Volcanes (La Palma)

The Ruta de los Volcanes is a spectacular hiking trail that traverses the volcanic ridge of La Palma, offering dramatic views of craters, lava fields, and pine forests. The trail starts at Refugio del Pilar and ends in the town of Fuencaliente, covering approximately 18 kilometers.

16.2.3 Roque Nublo (Gran Canaria)

Roque Nublo is an iconic volcanic rock formation and one of the most popular hiking destinations in Gran Canaria. The trail to the summit is relatively short but offers breathtaking views of the surrounding landscapes. The hike starts from the parking area near La Goleta and takes about 1.5 hours round trip.

16.3 Water Sports

16.3.1 Surfing (Fuerteventura)

Fuerteventura is renowned for its world-class surfing conditions, with consistent waves and a variety of breaks suitable for all levels. Popular spots include:

El Cotillo: Known for its powerful waves and consistent swells, making it ideal for experienced surfers.

Corralejo: Offers a range of breaks, from beginner-friendly beach breaks to more challenging reef breaks.

La Pared: A less crowded spot with strong waves and stunning coastal scenery.

16.3.2 Kitesurfing and Windsurfing (Tenerife and Gran Canaria)

The consistent trade winds make the Canary Islands a paradise for kitesurfing and windsurfing. Top spots include:

El Médano (Tenerife): Known for its reliable winds and excellent facilities, El Médano is a top destination for both kitesurfers and windsurfers.

Pozo Izquierdo (Gran Canaria): Famous for its strong winds and challenging conditions, Pozo Izquierdo hosts international windsurfing competitions and is ideal for advanced windsurfers.

16.3.3 Scuba Diving (El Hierro and Lanzarote)

The clear waters and diverse marine life of the Canary Islands make them a top destination for scuba diving. Notable dive sites include:

La Restinga (El Hierro): The marine reserve offers stunning underwater landscapes, including volcanic formations, caves, and a variety of marine species.

Museo Atlántico (Lanzarote): Europe's first underwater museum features sculptures by artist Jason deCaires Taylor, creating an artificial reef that attracts a wealth of marine life.

16.4 Climbing and Caving

16.4.1 Rock Climbing (Gran Canaria and Tenerife)

The volcanic rock formations of the Canary Islands provide excellent climbing opportunities. Popular climbing areas include:

Fataga (Gran Canaria): Offers a range of sport climbing routes with varying difficulty levels, set in a stunning mountainous landscape.

Arico (Tenerife): Known for its high-quality volcanic rock and extensive routes, Arico is a favorite among rock climbers.

16.4.2 Caving (Tenerife and Lanzarote)

Exploring the volcanic caves and lava tubes of the Canary Islands is an exciting adventure. Notable caving sites include:

Cueva del Viento (Tenerife): One of the longest lava tubes in the world, offering guided tours that explore its fascinating geological formations.

Cueva de los Verdes (Lanzarote): A spectacular cave system formed by lava flows, featuring guided tours that highlight its unique features and history.

16.5 Paragliding and Skydiving

16.5.1 Paragliding (Tenerife and La Palma)

The Canary Islands' dramatic landscapes and favorable weather conditions make them ideal for paragliding. Top spots include:

Izaña (Tenerife): Offering stunning views of Mount Teide and the surrounding landscape, Izaña is a popular launch site for paragliders.

Mirador de La Cumbrecita (La Palma): Known for its breathtaking views of the Caldera de Taburiente, this launch site provides an unforgettable paragliding experience.

16.5.2 Skydiving (Gran Canaria)

For those seeking the ultimate adrenaline rush, skydiving over the Canary Islands offers a thrilling experience with spectacular views. Gran Canaria is a popular destination for skydiving, with tandem jumps available for beginners and advanced jumps for experienced skydivers.

16.6 Cycling and Mountain Biking

16.6.1 Road Cycling (Tenerife and Gran Canaria)

The varied terrain and well-maintained roads of the Canary Islands make them a popular destination for road cycling. Notable routes include:

Mount Teide (Tenerife): The challenging ascent to Mount Teide is a favorite among cyclists, offering stunning views and a rewarding climb.

Valley of the Tears (Gran Canaria): Known for its steep climbs and dramatic scenery, this challenging route is a must-do for serious cyclists.

16.6.2 Mountain Biking (La Palma and Lanzarote)

The rugged landscapes of the Canary Islands provide excellent mountain biking opportunities. Popular trails include:

El Pilar to Fuencaliente (La Palma): This trail offers a mix of technical descents and scenic rides through pine forests and volcanic landscapes.

Timanfaya National Park (Lanzarote): The volcanic terrain and scenic trails of Timanfaya offer a unique mountain biking experience.

16.7 Wildlife and Nature Tours

16.7.1 Whale and Dolphin Watching (Various Islands)

The waters around the Canary Islands are home to several species of whales and dolphins, making it a prime destination for marine wildlife watching. Popular departure points include:

Los Cristianos (Tenerife): Regular boat tours offer the chance to see pilot whales and bottlenose dolphins.

Puerto Rico (Gran Canaria): Known for frequent sightings of various dolphin species and occasional whales.

La Palma: Offers excellent conditions for dolphin watching, with tours departing from Santa Cruz de La Palma.

16.7.2 Birdwatching (La Gomera and Fuerteventura)

The Canary Islands are a paradise for birdwatchers, with several endemic species and important migratory stopovers. Notable birdwatching spots include:

Garajonay National Park (La Gomera): Home to several endemic bird species, including the La Palma chaffinch and the Bolle's pigeon.

Jandía Natural Park (Fuerteventura): Known for its diverse birdlife, including the endangered houbara bustard and the Egyptian vulture.

16.8 Sailing and Boat Tours

16.8.1 Catamaran Tours (Tenerife and Gran Canaria)

Catamaran tours offer a relaxing way to explore the coastal waters of the Canary Islands. Highlights include:

Los Gigantes (Tenerife): Sail along the dramatic cliffs of Los Gigantes and enjoy snorkeling in the clear waters.

Maspalomas (Gran Canaria): Catamaran tours offer stunning views of the southern coast and opportunities for swimming and snorkeling.

16.8.2 Sailing Trips (Lanzarote and Fuerteventura)

For a more immersive experience, sailing trips allow you to explore the islands at a leisurely pace. Popular routes include:

Papagayo Beaches (Lanzarote): Sail to the beautiful Papagayo beaches and enjoy swimming, snorkeling, and sunbathing.

Isla de Lobos (Fuerteventura): A short sail to the uninhabited Isla de Lobos offers pristine beaches and excellent snorkeling opportunities.

16.9 Volunteering and Conservation Activities

16.9.1 Beach Cleanups

Participating in beach cleanups helps preserve the natural beauty of the Canary Islands and protect marine life. Many local organizations organize regular cleanups, and visitors are welcome to join.

16.9.2 Wildlife Monitoring

Volunteering with wildlife monitoring projects provides a unique opportunity to contribute to conservation efforts while experiencing the islands' natural beauty. Projects may involve monitoring bird populations, sea turtles, or marine mammals.

16.9.3 Habitat Restoration

Habitat restoration projects aim to protect and restore native ecosystems. Activities may include planting native species, removing invasive plants, and maintaining trails and facilities in protected areas.

Conclusion

The Canary Islands offer a diverse range of adventure activities that cater to thrill-seekers and nature lovers alike. From hiking and water sports to climbing and wildlife watching, the archipelago's unique landscapes and favorable climate provide endless opportunities for exciting and memorable experiences. By exploring the various adventure activities available across the islands, visitors can enjoy an action-packed vacation while appreciating the natural beauty and cultural richness of the Canary Islands. As we continue to explore the archipelago in the following chapters, the diverse offerings of each island will further illuminate the remarkable appeal of this destination.

Chapter 17: Wellness and Relaxation in the Canary Islands

17.1 Introduction to Wellness and Relaxation

The Canary Islands are not only a paradise for adventure seekers but also a haven for those seeking wellness and relaxation. The archipelago's mild climate, natural beauty, and abundance of spa facilities create the perfect environment for rejuvenation and self-care. This chapter explores the various wellness and relaxation options available across the Canary Islands, including spas, yoga retreats, thermal springs, and natural therapies.

17.2 Spa and Wellness Centers

17.2.1 Hotel Botánico & The Oriental Spa Garden (Tenerife)

Located in Puerto de la Cruz, Hotel Botánico & The Oriental Spa Garden is one of the top wellness destinations in Tenerife. The spa offers a range of treatments and facilities, including:

Thermal Circuit: Featuring saunas, steam baths, Jacuzzis, and an ice temple.

Treatment Rooms: Offering massages, facials, and body treatments inspired by Asian and European techniques.

Relaxation Areas: Beautiful gardens and tranquil areas for relaxation and meditation.

17.2.2 Lopesan Costa Meloneras Resort & Spa (Gran Canaria)

Lopesan Costa Meloneras Resort & Spa in Maspalomas, Gran Canaria, is renowned for its extensive wellness facilities. Highlights include:

Thalassotherapy Circuit: Utilizing seawater and marine elements for therapeutic treatments.

Hydrotherapy Pools: Heated pools with various hydro-massage jets.

Holistic Treatments: A range of therapies, including aromatherapy, reflexology, and Ayurvedic treatments.

17.2.3 Princesa Yaiza Suite Hotel Resort (Lanzarote)

Located in Playa Blanca, Lanzarote, Princesa Yaiza Suite Hotel Resort offers a luxurious spa experience. The Thalasso Center provides:

Marine Treatments: Utilizing seaweed and seawater for detoxifying and revitalizing therapies.

Spa Rituals: Combining traditional techniques with modern therapies for complete relaxation.

Beauty Treatments: A variety of facials, body wraps, and anti-aging treatments.

17.3 Yoga and Meditation Retreats

17.3.1 Surya Retreat (Fuerteventura)

Surya Retreat in Fuerteventura offers yoga and wellness retreats in a tranquil setting. The retreat focuses on holistic health and provides:

Daily Yoga Classes: Various styles, including Hatha, Vinyasa, and Yin Yoga.

Meditation Sessions: Guided meditation and mindfulness practices.

Nutritional Workshops: Healthy cooking classes and nutritional advice.

17.3.2 Azulfit Yoga & Pilates Retreat (Fuerteventura)

Azulfit Yoga & Pilates Retreat offers a combination of yoga, Pilates, and wellness programs. The retreat features:

Yoga and Pilates Classes: Suitable for all levels, with experienced instructors.

Holistic Therapies: Massages, Reiki, and holistic treatments.

Healthy Cuisine: Nutritious meals prepared with fresh, local ingredients.

17.3.3 EcoYoga Retreat (La Gomera)

Located in the lush landscapes of La Gomera, EcoYoga Retreat provides a peaceful environment for yoga and meditation. The retreat emphasizes sustainability and natural living, offering:

Eco-Friendly Accommodation: Rustic yet comfortable lodging in harmony with nature.

Outdoor Yoga Sessions: Classes held in beautiful natural settings.

Organic Meals: Delicious, plant-based meals sourced from local organic farms.

17.4 Thermal Springs and Natural Pools

17.4.1 La Fajana Natural Pools (La Palma)

La Fajana Natural Pools are located in the northeast of La Palma, offering a unique and relaxing experience. These natural pools are formed by volcanic rock and filled with seawater, providing a refreshing place to swim and unwind.

17.4.2 Caldeira Velha (Tenerife)

Caldeira Velha is a natural thermal spring located in the north of Tenerife. The warm, mineral-rich waters are surrounded by lush vegetation, creating a serene and rejuvenating environment. Visitors can enjoy the therapeutic benefits of the thermal waters while soaking in the natural beauty of the surroundings.

17.4.3 Pozo de la Salud (El Hierro)

Pozo de la Salud is a natural spa located in the El Golfo Valley of El Hierro. The spa is known for its mineral-rich waters, believed to have therapeutic properties. Visitors can enjoy a range of treatments, including hydrotherapy, mud baths, and mineral soaks, all designed to promote relaxation and well-being.

17.5 Natural Therapies and Alternative Treatments

17.5.1 Aloe Vera Treatments

The Canary Islands are known for their high-quality aloe vera, which is used in various natural therapies and treatments. Aloe vera is known for its soothing, moisturizing, and healing properties, making it ideal for skincare treatments such as:

Aloe Vera Facials: Using fresh aloe vera gel to hydrate and rejuvenate the skin.

Aloe Vera Body Wraps: Detoxifying and nourishing treatments that leave the skin soft and refreshed.

Aloe Vera Massages: Incorporating aloe vera gel to soothe and heal the skin while providing a relaxing massage experience.

17.5.2 Volcanic Stone Therapy

Volcanic stone therapy utilizes heated volcanic stones to provide a deeply relaxing and therapeutic massage. The stones' heat penetrates the muscles, helping to release tension and promote circulation. Many spas across the Canary Islands offer this treatment, which is particularly beneficial for:

Muscle Relaxation: Easing muscle tension and stiffness.

Stress Relief: Promoting a sense of calm and relaxation.

Improved Circulation: Enhancing blood flow and detoxification.

17.5.3 Thalassotherapy

Thalassotherapy harnesses the healing properties of seawater and marine elements, such as seaweed and algae, for therapeutic treatments. The Canary Islands' coastal location makes them ideal for thalassotherapy, which can include:

Marine Baths: Soaking in mineral-rich seawater to promote relaxation and skin health.

Seaweed Wraps: Detoxifying and nourishing treatments using fresh seaweed.

Hydrotherapy: Utilizing water jets and underwater massages to relieve muscle tension and improve circulation.

17.6 Outdoor Relaxation Activities

17.6.1 Beach Relaxation

The Canary Islands boast numerous beautiful beaches, perfect for relaxing and unwinding. Some of the best beaches for relaxation include:

Playa de Las Teresitas (Tenerife): A golden sandy beach with calm waters, ideal for swimming and sunbathing.

Playa de Papagayo (Lanzarote): Secluded coves with crystal-clear waters, perfect for a peaceful day by the sea.

Playa de Sotavento (Fuerteventura): A long stretch of sandy beach with shallow lagoons, ideal for relaxing walks and gentle swims.

17.6.2 Nature Walks and Forest Bathing

Connecting with nature through gentle walks and forest bathing can provide a sense of peace and well-being. The Canary Islands offer numerous trails and natural areas for outdoor relaxation, including:

Anaga Rural Park (Tenerife): Lush laurel forests and scenic trails, perfect for peaceful walks and nature immersion.

Bosque de Los Tilos (La Palma): A beautiful laurel forest with well-marked trails, ideal for forest bathing and relaxation.

Garajonay National Park (La Gomera): Ancient forests and serene paths, offering a tranquil escape into nature.

17.6.3 Stargazing

The clear skies and minimal light pollution of the Canary Islands make them one of the best destinations in the world for stargazing. Some top stargazing spots include:

Teide National Park (Tenerife): High-altitude views and clear skies make this an ideal location for observing stars, planets, and constellations.

Roque de los Muchachos Observatory (La Palma): Home to one of the world's leading astronomical observatories, offering unparalleled stargazing opportunities.

Mirador de Morro Velosa (Fuerteventura): A scenic viewpoint with minimal light pollution, perfect for a night of stargazing.

Conclusion

The Canary Islands offer a wide range of wellness and relaxation options, making them an ideal destination for those seeking to rejuvenate their mind, body, and spirit. From luxurious spa treatments and yoga retreats to natural therapies and serene outdoor activities, the archipelago provides endless opportunities for relaxation and self-care. By exploring the various wellness and relaxation options available across the islands, visitors can enjoy a truly restorative and enriching experience. As we continue to explore the Canary Islands in the following chapters, the diverse offerings of each island will further illuminate the remarkable appeal of this destination.

Chapter 18: Gastronomic Experiences in the Canary Islands

18.1 Introduction to Canary Island Cuisine

The Canary Islands boast a rich culinary tradition that reflects a blend of Spanish, African, and Latin American influences. The local cuisine is known for its simplicity, freshness, and flavorful ingredients. This chapter explores the diverse gastronomic experiences available in the Canary Islands, highlighting traditional dishes, culinary tours, food festivals, and the best places to savor authentic Canarian flavors.

18.2 Traditional Dishes

18.2.1 Papas Arrugadas with Mojo

Papas arrugadas, or "wrinkled potatoes," are small, unpeeled potatoes boiled in heavily salted water until they form a wrinkled skin. They are typically served with two types of mojo sauce:

Mojo Rojo: A red sauce made from red peppers, garlic, cumin, olive oil, and vinegar, often with a spicy kick.

Mojo Verde: A green sauce made from green peppers, cilantro, garlic, cumin, olive oil, and vinegar, offering a milder, herbaceous flavor.

18.2.2 Sancocho Canario

Sancocho Canario is a traditional fish stew made with salted fish (typically grouper or wreckfish), potatoes, and sweet potatoes. It is usually accompanied by gofio (toasted grain flour) and mojo sauce, creating a hearty and flavorful dish.

18.2.3 Gofio

Gofio is a versatile flour made from roasted grains, such as maize or wheat. It is a staple in Canarian cuisine and can be used in various forms, such as:

Gofio Escaldado: A thick paste made by mixing gofio with fish broth or milk.

Gofio Mousse: A sweet dessert mousse made with gofio, honey, and almonds.

Gofio in Soups and Stews: Used as a thickener to add a distinct nutty flavor.

18.2.4 Bienmesabe

Bienmesabe, meaning "tastes good to me," is a traditional Canarian dessert made from ground almonds, honey, sugar, and eggs. It has a rich, sweet flavor and is often served with ice cream or as a filling for cakes and pastries.

18.3 Culinary Tours and Experiences

18.3.1 Wine Tasting Tours

The Canary Islands are known for their unique volcanic wines, with several vineyards offering tours and tastings.

18.3.1.1 Bodegas Monje (Tenerife)

Located in El Sauzal, Bodegas Monje offers guided tours of their vineyards and wine cellars, followed by tastings of their red, white, and rosé wines. The tour also includes a visit to the winery's restaurant, where visitors can enjoy traditional Canarian dishes paired with their wines.

18.3.1.2 Bodegas El Grifo (Lanzarote)

Bodegas El Grifo, one of the oldest wineries in the Canary Islands, is located in the La Geria region of Lanzarote. The winery offers tours of its vineyards, wine museum, and production facilities, followed by tastings of their award-winning wines.

18.3.2 Market Tours

Exploring local markets is a great way to experience the vibrant food culture of the Canary Islands.

18.3.2.1 Mercado de Nuestra Señora de África (Tenerife)

Located in Santa Cruz de Tenerife, this bustling market offers a wide variety of fresh produce, seafood, meats, cheeses, and local delicacies. Guided tours are available to provide insights into the market's history and the local food culture.

18.3.2.2 Mercado de Vegueta (Gran Canaria)

Situated in the historic district of Las Palmas, this market is known for its colorful stalls selling fresh fruits, vegetables, fish, meats, and traditional Canarian products. Visitors can take guided tours to learn about the market's offerings and sample local specialties.

18.3.3 Cooking Classes

Taking a cooking class is a fantastic way to learn how to prepare traditional Canarian dishes.

18.3.3.1 Canary Cooking Experience (Gran Canaria)

This cooking school offers hands-on classes where participants can learn to make a variety of Canarian dishes, such as papas arrugadas, sancocho, and bienmesabe. The classes include a visit to a local market to source fresh ingredients.

18.3.3.2 Cocina en Casa (Tenerife)

Cocina en Casa offers personalized cooking classes in a home setting, focusing on traditional Canarian recipes and techniques. Participants can enjoy a relaxed, intimate environment while learning to prepare and savor local dishes.

18.4 Food Festivals and Events

18.4.1 Fiesta de San Andrés (Tenerife)

The Fiesta de San Andrés is celebrated in the town of Icod de los Vinos in Tenerife on November 29th. The festival is known for its wine tasting and traditional foods, such as roasted chestnuts and sweet potatoes. Visitors can enjoy local wines and experience the lively atmosphere of this cultural event.

18.4.2 Wine Run Lanzarote

The Wine Run Lanzarote is an annual event that combines a half-marathon and a 12K race through the picturesque vineyards of Lanzarote's La Geria region. The event includes wine tastings, food stalls, and live music, making it a unique celebration of the island's wine culture.

18.4.3 Saborea Lanzarote

Saborea Lanzarote is a food and wine festival held annually in the town of Teguise. The event showcases the island's culinary diversity, with tastings of local dishes, wines, and products. Visitors can participate in cooking workshops, attend presentations by renowned chefs, and enjoy live entertainment.

18.5 Best Places to Eat

18.5.1 El Rincón de Juan Carlos (Tenerife)

El Rincón de Juan Carlos, located in Los Gigantes, is a Michelin-starred restaurant renowned for its creative cuisine and exceptional service. The menu features innovative dishes that highlight the flavors of the Canary Islands, using locally sourced ingredients.

18.5.2 La Tegala (Lanzarote)

La Tegala in Macher, Lanzarote, offers a fine dining experience with a focus on traditional Canarian flavors and modern culinary techniques. The restaurant's tasting menu showcases seasonal ingredients and local specialties, complemented by an extensive wine list.

18.5.3 Restaurante Casa Marcos (Fuerteventura)

Located in Villaverde, Restaurante Casa Marcos is a popular eatery known for its authentic Canarian cuisine and warm, welcoming atmosphere. The menu features traditional dishes such as goat stew, grilled seafood, and papas arrugadas, all made with fresh, local ingredients.

18.5.4 El Jardín de la Sal (La Palma)

El Jardín de la Sal is situated in the salt flats of Fuencaliente, offering a unique dining experience with stunning views of the Atlantic Ocean. The menu focuses on fresh seafood and local specialties, with a strong emphasis on sustainability and seasonal ingredients.

18.5.5 Casa Domínguez (La Gomera)

Located in San Sebastián de La Gomera, Casa Domínguez is a charming restaurant that offers traditional Gomeran cuisine. The menu includes dishes such as almogrote (a cheese spread), watercress soup, and grilled meats, all served in a cozy, rustic setting.

18.6 Street Food and Local Specialties

18.6.1 Churros with Chocolate

Churros, a popular Spanish treat, are also a favorite in the Canary Islands. These deep-fried dough pastries are often enjoyed with a cup of rich, thick hot chocolate for dipping. Street vendors and local cafes serve churros throughout the islands, making them a perfect snack or dessert.

18.6.2 Arepas

Arepas, cornmeal patties filled with various ingredients such as cheese, meats, and vegetables, are a popular street food in the Canary Islands. Originating from Venezuela, arepas have become a staple in the local food scene and can be found at food stalls and casual eateries.

18.6.3 Bocadillos

Bocadillos are Spanish-style sandwiches made with crusty bread and filled with a variety of ingredients, such as cured ham, cheese, tuna, and peppers. These tasty sandwiches are widely available at bakeries, cafes, and street vendors, offering a quick and satisfying meal on the go.

Conclusion

The Canary Islands offer a rich and diverse gastronomic experience, from traditional dishes and culinary tours to food festivals and fine dining. By exploring the local cuisine and participating in culinary activities, visitors can gain a deeper appreciation of the islands' cultural heritage and culinary traditions. As we continue to explore the Canary Islands in the following chapters, the diverse offerings of each island will further illuminate the remarkable appeal of this destination.

Chapter 19: Art and Culture in the Canary Islands

19.1 Introduction to Art and Culture

The Canary Islands boast a vibrant and diverse cultural scene, deeply rooted in their unique history and geographical location. The archipelago has been a melting pot of influences from Europe, Africa, and Latin America, resulting in a rich tapestry of artistic expression. This chapter explores the art and cultural offerings of the Canary Islands, including museums, galleries, festivals, and traditional crafts that showcase the islands' heritage and contemporary creativity.

19.2 Museums and Art Galleries

19.2.1 TEA Tenerife Espacio de las Artes (Tenerife)

Located in Santa Cruz de Tenerife, TEA Tenerife Espacio de las Artes is a contemporary art center that houses a diverse collection of modern and contemporary art. Highlights include:

Permanent Collection: Featuring works by notable Canarian artists such as Óscar Domínguez and contemporary pieces by international artists.

Temporary Exhibitions: Regularly rotating exhibits that showcase cutting-edge art from around the world.

Public Programs: Workshops, lectures, and film screenings that engage the community in the arts.

19.2.2 CAAM (Centro Atlántico de Arte Moderno) (Gran Canaria)

CAAM in Las Palmas, Gran Canaria, is a leading institution for modern and contemporary art in the Canary Islands. The museum focuses on the cultural connections between Europe, Africa, and Latin America, and features:

Permanent Collection: Artworks by prominent Canarian and international artists, emphasizing transatlantic cultural exchanges.

Temporary Exhibitions: Showcasing contemporary art from around the world.

Educational Programs: Workshops, guided tours, and art education initiatives for all ages.

19.2.3 Fundación César Manrique (Lanzarote)

The Fundación César Manrique in Tahíche, Lanzarote, is dedicated to the life and work of César Manrique, a visionary artist and architect who played a pivotal role in shaping Lanzarote's aesthetic landscape. The foundation features:

Art and Architecture: Manrique's home, built into a volcanic landscape, showcases his unique integration of art and nature.

Permanent Collection: Works by Manrique and other contemporary artists.

Cultural Programs: Exhibitions, workshops, and events that promote Manrique's legacy and environmental philosophy.

19.2.4 Museo Internacional de Arte Contemporáneo (MIAC) (Lanzarote)

Located in the historic Castillo de San José in Arrecife, MIAC features a significant collection of contemporary art. The museum offers:

Permanent Collection: Works by Canarian and international artists, focusing on modern and contemporary art.

Temporary Exhibitions: Regularly changing exhibits that highlight various artistic movements and styles.

Restaurant: A dining experience with panoramic views of the harbor, designed by César Manrique.

19.3 Traditional Crafts and Artisans

19.3.1 Pottery

Traditional Canarian pottery is characterized by its unique designs and techniques passed down through generations. Key locations to explore pottery include:

La Atalaya (Gran Canaria): Known for its handcrafted pottery made without a potter's wheel, a technique dating back to the island's indigenous people.

Calle Real de La Cruz (La Palma): A hub for traditional pottery workshops and stores.

19.3.2 Embroidery and Lace

Intricate embroidery and lacework are hallmarks of Canarian craftsmanship. These delicate textiles are used in traditional clothing, table linens, and decorative items. Notable places to find these crafts include:

Villa de Mazo (La Palma): Famous for its lace and embroidery, with several shops and workshops showcasing these beautiful crafts.

La Orotava (Tenerife): A town known for its traditional embroideries, particularly during the Corpus Christi celebrations when intricate floral carpets are created.

19.3.3 Basketry

Basket weaving is a traditional craft practiced throughout the Canary Islands, using local materials such as palm leaves, reed, and willow. Baskets are crafted for both practical and decorative purposes. Notable locations include:

El Hierro: Known for its robust and functional basketry, often used in agricultural practices.

La Gomera: Renowned for its intricate basket designs made from palm leaves.

19.4 Music and Dance

19.4.1 Folklore and Traditional Music

Traditional Canarian music is an essential part of the islands' cultural identity, featuring instruments such as the timple (a small stringed instrument) and incorporating various dance styles. Key music and dance forms include:

Isa: A lively folk dance performed at festivals and celebrations.

Folia: A slower, more melancholic style of music and dance.

Malagueñas: A style of folk music with influences from Andalusia.

19.4.2 Modern Music and Festivals

The Canary Islands also have a vibrant contemporary music scene, with numerous festivals showcasing a range of genres from jazz to electronic music. Notable festivals include:

Canary Islands Music Festival: An annual classical music festival held across various venues in the islands, featuring performances by renowned international and local artists.

Festival Internacional de Jazz de Canarias: A popular jazz festival attracting musicians from around the world, held in stunning outdoor settings.

19.4.3 Traditional Festivals

Festivals play a crucial role in the cultural life of the Canary Islands, often featuring music, dance, and traditional customs. Important festivals include:

Carnival (Various Islands): The Carnival of Santa Cruz de Tenerife is one of the largest and most spectacular carnivals in the world, featuring parades, music, dance, and elaborate costumes. Other islands also celebrate carnival with their own unique flair.

Fiesta de San Juan (Various Islands): Celebrated on June 24th, this festival marks the summer solstice with bonfires, fireworks, and various festivities.

Bajada de la Virgen de los Reyes (El Hierro): Held every four years, this pilgrimage honors the island's patron saint with a procession, traditional music, and dance.

19.5 Literature and Theatre

19.5.1 Canarian Literature

The Canary Islands have a rich literary tradition, with several notable authors who have contributed to Spanish literature. Key figures include:

Benito Pérez Galdós: A prolific novelist and playwright from Gran Canaria, known for his works depicting Spanish society in the 19th century.

Tomás Morales: A poet from Gran Canaria, celebrated for his modernist poetry that reflects the beauty of the islands.

19.5.2 Theatre and Performing Arts

Theatre and performing arts are integral to the cultural scene in the Canary Islands, with numerous venues hosting a variety of performances. Important theatres include:

Teatro Guimerá (Tenerife): Located in Santa Cruz de Tenerife, this historic theatre hosts a wide range of performances, including plays, concerts, and dance shows.

Teatro Pérez Galdós (Gran Canaria): Situated in Las Palmas, this theatre is a hub for performing arts, featuring opera, theatre, and classical music concerts.

19.6 Street Art and Public Installations

The Canary Islands are also known for their vibrant street art and public installations, which add a contemporary edge to the cultural landscape. Notable examples include:

La Laguna (Tenerife): This UNESCO World Heritage site features numerous street art murals that celebrate the town's history and culture.

Las Palmas (Gran Canaria): The city's urban areas are adorned with colorful murals and public art installations, reflecting its dynamic cultural scene.

Conclusion

The Canary Islands offer a rich and diverse cultural experience, encompassing traditional crafts, music, dance, literature, and contemporary art. By exploring the various cultural offerings, visitors can gain a deeper understanding of the islands' unique heritage and artistic expression. As we continue to explore the Canary Islands in the following chapters, the diverse offerings of each island will further illuminate the remarkable appeal of this destination.

Chapter 20: Nightlife and Entertainment in the Canary Islands

20.1 Introduction to Nightlife

The Canary Islands are known for their vibrant nightlife and diverse entertainment options, offering something for everyone, from lively nightclubs and beach bars to sophisticated lounges and cultural performances. This chapter explores the best nightlife and entertainment experiences across the archipelago, ensuring that visitors can enjoy their evenings to the fullest, regardless of their preferences.

20.2 Nightclubs and Dance Venues

20.2.1 Papagayo Beach Club (Tenerife)

Located in Playa de las Américas, Papagayo Beach Club is one of the most popular nightlife destinations in Tenerife. The club features:

Open-Air Dance Floor: With stunning views of the ocean.

Top DJs: Playing a mix of house, electronic, and popular music.

VIP Areas: Offering exclusive service and premium seating.

20.2.2 Pacha (Gran Canaria)

Pacha in Playa del Inglés, Gran Canaria, is part of the famous global nightclub brand known for its high-energy atmosphere and international DJs. Highlights include:

Large Dance Floor: Designed for dancing the night away.

Themed Nights: Featuring different music genres and special performances.

Rooftop Terrace: Offering a more relaxed setting with beautiful views.

20.2.3 Aqua Club (Fuerteventura)

Aqua Club in Corralejo, Fuerteventura, is a popular venue for both locals and tourists. The club offers:

Eclectic Music: From Latin beats to electronic dance music.

Live Performances: Including local bands and international acts.

Stylish Decor: Creating a chic and inviting atmosphere.

20.3 Beach Bars and Lounges

20.3.1 Kaluna Beach Club (Tenerife)

Located in Costa Adeje, Kaluna Beach Club is a stylish beachside venue offering a laid-back atmosphere during the day and lively parties at night. Features include:

Infinity Pool: Overlooking the ocean, perfect for a refreshing dip.

Sun Loungers and Cabanas: Ideal for relaxing and soaking up the sun.

Live DJs: Providing a soundtrack of chill-out tunes and dance music.

20.3.2 Amadores Beach Club (Gran Canaria)

Amadores Beach Club in Puerto Rico, Gran Canaria, is a luxurious beach club known for its relaxed vibe and stunning views. Highlights include:

Heated Pools: Surrounded by sun loungers and Balinese beds.

Gourmet Dining: Offering a menu of fresh seafood and international cuisine.

Cocktail Bar: Serving a wide range of signature cocktails and fine wines.

20.3.3 La Concha (Lanzarote)

La Concha in Arrecife, Lanzarote, is a trendy beach bar that transforms into a lively nightspot after dark. Features include:

Oceanfront Setting: With stunning views of the Atlantic Ocean.

Live Music: Featuring local bands and acoustic performances.

Cocktail Specials: A variety of creative and classic cocktails.

20.4 Live Music and Cultural Performances

20.4.1 Auditorio de Tenerife (Tenerife)

Located in Santa Cruz de Tenerife, the Auditorio de Tenerife is a world-class venue for live music and cultural performances. Highlights include:

Classical Concerts: Featuring performances by the Tenerife Symphony Orchestra.

Opera and Ballet: Regular productions showcasing local and international talent.

Jazz and World Music: Concerts and festivals celebrating diverse musical genres.

20.4.2 Alfredo Kraus Auditorium (Gran Canaria)

The Alfredo Kraus Auditorium in Las Palmas, Gran Canaria, is a premier venue for concerts and cultural events. Highlights include:

Symphonic Performances: Featuring the Gran Canaria Philharmonic Orchestra.

Film Screenings: Part of various film festivals hosted at the auditorium.

Cultural Festivals: Including the Canary Islands Music Festival and the International Jazz Festival.

20.4.3 Casa de la Cultura Agüimes (Gran Canaria)

Casa de la Cultura Agüimes in Gran Canaria offers a range of cultural performances and events. Highlights include:

Theatre Productions: Featuring local and international plays.

Dance Performances: Showcasing traditional and contemporary dance.

Art Exhibitions: Displaying works by local artists and photographers.

20.5 Casinos and Gaming

20.5.1 Casino Santa Cruz (Tenerife)

Located in Santa Cruz de Tenerife, Casino Santa Cruz offers a sophisticated gaming experience with:

Table Games: Including blackjack, roulette, and poker.

Slot Machines: A wide variety of options for casual gamers.

Entertainment: Live music, performances, and special events.

20.5.2 Casino Las Palmas (Gran Canaria)

Casino Las Palmas in Gran Canaria is a popular destination for gaming and entertainment. Features include:

Gaming Tables: Offering a range of classic casino games.

Poker Tournaments: Regularly scheduled events attracting players from around the world.

Dining and Bars: A restaurant and bars offering delicious food and drinks.

20.5.3 Gran Casino Costa Meloneras (Gran Canaria)

Located in Maspalomas, Gran Canaria, Gran Casino Costa Meloneras is a stylish casino offering:

Wide Range of Games: Including poker, blackjack, roulette, and slot machines.

Live Entertainment: Regular shows and musical performances.

Upscale Atmosphere: A luxurious setting for an evening of gaming and fun.

20.6 Themed Bars and Pubs

20.6.1 The Irish Rover (Gran Canaria)

Located in Playa del Inglés, The Irish Rover is a popular Irish pub known for its lively atmosphere and friendly staff. Highlights include:

Live Music: Regular performances by local and visiting bands.

Traditional Irish Fare: Including Guinness, Irish whiskey, and classic pub food.

Sports Screenings: Live broadcasts of major sporting events.

20.6.2 The Roof (Tenerife)

The Roof in Costa Adeje, Tenerife, is a trendy rooftop bar offering panoramic views and a chic atmosphere. Features include:

Cocktail Menu: A wide range of creative cocktails and premium spirits.

Live DJs: Providing a soundtrack of chill-out and dance music.

Sunset Views: Perfect for enjoying a drink while watching the sun set over the ocean.

20.6.3 Rock Island Bar (Fuerteventura)

Located in Corralejo, Rock Island Bar is a laid-back venue known for its live music and relaxed vibe. Highlights include:

Acoustic Sessions: Regular performances by local and visiting musicians.

Craft Beers and Cocktails: A selection of artisanal drinks.

Intimate Setting: A cozy and welcoming atmosphere.

20.7 Late-Night Dining

20.7.1 La Cazuela (Tenerife)

La Cazuela in Santa Cruz de Tenerife is a popular spot for late-night dining, offering a menu of traditional Canarian dishes and Spanish tapas. Highlights include:

Tapas Selection: A variety of small plates perfect for sharing.

Seafood Specials: Freshly caught seafood prepared with local ingredients.

Relaxed Atmosphere: A cozy setting for a late-night meal.

20.7.2 Restaurante La Cascada (Gran Canaria)

Located in Maspalomas, Restaurante La Cascada offers late-night dining in an elegant setting. Features include:

Mediterranean Cuisine: A menu featuring fresh, locally sourced ingredients.

Extensive Wine List: A selection of local and international wines.

Outdoor Terrace: A beautiful setting for an al fresco meal.

20.7.3 El Diablo (Lanzarote)

Situated in Timanfaya National Park, El Diablo is a unique restaurant that uses geothermal heat to cook its dishes. The restaurant offers:

Volcanic Grill: Meat and seafood cooked over a volcanic vent.

Local Dishes: Traditional Canarian cuisine with a twist.

Spectacular Views: Panoramic views of the volcanic landscape.

Conclusion

The Canary Islands offer a vibrant and diverse nightlife and entertainment scene, catering to all tastes and preferences. From high-energy nightclubs and beach bars to sophisticated lounges and cultural performances, there is something for everyone to enjoy. By exploring the various nightlife and entertainment options available across the islands, visitors can experience the lively spirit and rich cultural heritage of the Canary Islands. As we continue to explore the archipelago in the following chapters, the diverse offerings of each island will further illuminate the remarkable appeal of this destination.

Chapter 21: Exploring the Natural Wonders of the Canary Islands

21.1 Introduction to Natural Wonders

The Canary Islands are a treasure trove of natural wonders, boasting diverse landscapes that range from volcanic mountains and lush forests to pristine beaches and dramatic cliffs. This chapter delves into the breathtaking natural attractions across the archipelago, offering insights into the unique geological formations, rich biodiversity, and stunning scenery that make the Canary Islands a paradise for nature lovers.

21.2 Volcanic Landscapes

21.2.1 Teide National Park (Tenerife)

Teide National Park is home to Mount Teide, Spain's highest peak and one of the most iconic landmarks in the Canary Islands. The park features:

Mount Teide: Standing at 3,718 meters, this dormant volcano offers breathtaking views and a challenging hike. The summit can be reached by cable car, followed by a short but strenuous hike.

Lunar Landscape: Unique rock formations and volcanic terrain that resemble the surface of the moon.

Stargazing: Teide National Park is renowned for its clear skies and is a prime location for stargazing, with several observatories in the area.

21.2.2 Timanfaya National Park (Lanzarote)

Timanfaya National Park is famous for its otherworldly volcanic landscapes, formed by eruptions in the 18th century. Highlights include:

Montañas del Fuego (Fire Mountains): A series of volcanic craters and lava fields that showcase the power of volcanic activity.

Geothermal Demonstrations: Visitors can witness the intense heat just below the surface, with demonstrations such as water turning to steam instantly and dry brush catching fire.

El Diablo Restaurant: A unique dining experience where food is cooked using geothermal heat.

21.2.3 La Palma Volcanic Ridge (La Palma)

La Palma's volcanic ridge offers spectacular hiking opportunities and stunning views of the island's volcanic landscape. Key attractions include:

Ruta de los Volcanes: A challenging hiking trail that traverses the island's volcanic ridge, offering panoramic views of craters, lava fields, and the surrounding ocean.

Volcán de San Antonio: An accessible volcano with a visitor center and a short trail around its crater, providing insights into the island's volcanic activity.

21.3 Lush Forests and Biodiversity

21.3.1 Garajonay National Park (La Gomera)

Garajonay National Park is a UNESCO World Heritage site known for its ancient laurel forests. The park features:

Laurisilva Forest: A dense, misty forest that dates back to the Tertiary period, offering a glimpse into prehistoric ecosystems.

El Cedro Forest: A lush, green area with numerous hiking trails and scenic viewpoints.

Endemic Species: The park is home to several endemic plant and animal species, making it a biodiversity hotspot.

21.3.2 Anaga Rural Park (Tenerife)

Located in the northeastern part of Tenerife, Anaga Rural Park is a lush, green area known for its rich biodiversity and dramatic landscapes. Highlights include:

Laurisilva Forest: Similar to Garajonay, Anaga boasts ancient laurel forests with well-marked trails.

Scenic Trails: Popular hikes such as the Path of the Senses, which offer stunning views and a sensory experience of the forest.

Unique Flora and Fauna: Home to several endemic species, including the Tenerife blue chaffinch and various unique plant species.

21.3.3 Los Tilos (La Palma)

Los Tilos is a lush laurel forest located in the northeastern part of La Palma. The area features:

Bosque de Los Tilos: A dense, green forest with numerous trails and scenic viewpoints.

Cascada de Los Tilos: A beautiful waterfall accessible via a short hike, providing a refreshing natural attraction.

Biodiversity: The forest is home to a variety of plant and animal species, making it a great spot for nature enthusiasts.

21.4 Pristine Beaches and Coastal Scenery

21.4.1 Playa de Las Teresitas (Tenerife)

Playa de Las Teresitas is one of Tenerife's most beautiful beaches, known for its golden sands and calm, turquoise waters. Features include:

Imported Sand: The beach is made of sand imported from the Sahara Desert, giving it a unique appearance.

Safe Swimming: The calm waters and lifeguard presence make it ideal for families and safe swimming.

Facilities: Amenities such as sunbeds, umbrellas, and beachside cafes enhance the visitor experience.

21.4.2 Papagayo Beaches (Lanzarote)

The Papagayo Beaches are a series of pristine coves located in the Los Ajaches Natural Park, offering:

Crystal-Clear Waters: Ideal for swimming, snorkeling, and enjoying the marine life.

Secluded Coves: The beaches are relatively untouched and provide a sense of tranquility and seclusion.

Stunning Scenery: Surrounded by volcanic cliffs and natural landscapes.

21.4.3 Maspalomas Dunes (Gran Canaria)

The Maspalomas Dunes are a unique coastal landscape located in the south of Gran Canaria. Highlights include:

Dune System: A vast area of shifting sand dunes that resemble a mini desert.

Nature Reserve: The dunes are part of a protected nature reserve, home to various plant and animal species.

Lagoon and Lighthouse: The area includes a scenic lagoon (La Charca) and the historic Maspalomas Lighthouse.

21.5 Dramatic Cliffs and Rock Formations

21.5.1 Los Gigantes (Tenerife)

Los Gigantes are massive cliffs located on the western coast of Tenerife. Features include:

Towering Cliffs: The cliffs rise up to 800 meters above sea level, providing a dramatic backdrop.

Boat Tours: Visitors can take boat tours to see the cliffs up close and spot marine life such as dolphins and whales.

Scenic Viewpoints: Several viewpoints along the coast offer stunning views of the cliffs and the ocean.

21.5.2 Roque Nublo (Gran Canaria)

Roque Nublo is an iconic volcanic rock formation in the center of Gran Canaria. Highlights include:

Natural Monument: Roque Nublo is a symbol of Gran Canaria and a popular hiking destination.

Panoramic Views: The hike to the top offers breathtaking views of the surrounding landscapes and, on clear days, views of Mount Teide on Tenerife.

Geological Significance: The rock formation is a remnant of ancient volcanic activity.

21.5.3 Roque de los Muchachos (La Palma)

Roque de los Muchachos is the highest point on La Palma and one of the best spots for stargazing. Features include:

Observatories: Home to one of the world's leading astronomical observatories, taking advantage of the clear skies and minimal light pollution.

Spectacular Views: Panoramic views of the island and the ocean from the summit.

Astronomical Tours: Guided tours and stargazing sessions available for visitors.

21.6 Unique Geological Features

21.6.1 La Cueva del Viento (Tenerife)

La Cueva del Viento is one of the longest lava tubes in the world, located in the north of Tenerife. Highlights include:

Guided Tours: Explore the underground tunnels and learn about the geological processes that formed them.

Unique Lava Formations: Fascinating features such as lava stalactites, lava lakes, and unique fauna.

Educational Experience: Interpretive center providing information about volcanic activity and the island's geology.

21.6.2 Los Hervideros (Lanzarote)

Los Hervideros is a series of dramatic cliffs and volcanic caves formed by the cooling of lava as it met the ocean. Features include:

Spectacular Waves: Waves crash into the cliffs and caves, creating impressive displays of natural power.

Scenic Walkways: Pathways and viewing platforms allow visitors to safely enjoy the scenery.

Photography Opportunities: The rugged coastline and dynamic waves make for stunning photographs.

21.6.3 Charco de los Clicos (Lanzarote)

Charco de los Clicos, also known as the Green Lagoon, is a striking natural feature located near the village of El Golfo. Highlights include:

Green Lagoon: The vivid green color of the lagoon is caused by the presence of algae and sulfur, contrasting sharply with the black volcanic sand.

Volcanic Beach: The beach around the lagoon is composed of black volcanic sand, adding to the dramatic landscape.

Scenic Trails: Walking trails around the area offer views of the lagoon and the surrounding volcanic landscape.

21.7 Marine Life and Underwater Wonders

21.7.1 Diving in La Restinga Marine Reserve (El Hierro)

La Restinga Marine Reserve is one of the top diving destinations in Europe, located off the coast of El Hierro. Highlights include:

Diverse Marine Life: Rich biodiversity, including barracudas, rays, and various species of fish.

Volcanic Underwater Landscapes: Fascinating rock formations, lava flows, and underwater caves.

Diving Schools: Several dive centers offer courses and guided dives for all levels.

21.7.2 Snorkeling in El Cabrón Marine Reserve (Gran Canaria)

El Cabrón Marine Reserve is a popular snorkeling and diving spot in Gran Canaria. Features include:

Clear Waters: Excellent visibility for observing marine life.

Rich Biodiversity: A variety of fish species, octopuses, and other marine creatures.

Accessible Sites: Easy entry points for snorkelers and divers of all experience levels.

21.7.3 Whale and Dolphin Watching (Tenerife and La Gomera)

The waters around the Canary Islands are home to several species of whales and dolphins, making it a prime location for marine wildlife watching. Popular departure points include:

Los Cristianos (Tenerife): Regular boat tours offering the chance to see pilot whales and bottlenose dolphins.

San Sebastián (La Gomera): Tours departing from the capital, offering opportunities to see various dolphin species and occasionally whales.

Conclusion

The Canary Islands are a haven for nature enthusiasts, offering an incredible array of natural wonders that span volcanic landscapes, lush forests, pristine beaches, and dramatic cliffs. By exploring these breathtaking natural attractions, visitors can experience the diverse beauty and unique geological features that make the Canary Islands a truly remarkable destination. As we continue to explore the archipelago in the following chapters, the diverse offerings of each island will further illuminate the remarkable appeal of this destination.

Chapter 22: Island-Hopping Adventures in the Canary Islands

22.1 Introduction to Island-Hopping

One of the most exciting ways to explore the Canary Islands is through island-hopping. Each island boasts its own unique landscapes, culture, and attractions, making it a fascinating adventure to travel between them. This chapter provides a comprehensive guide to island-hopping in the Canary Islands, including transportation options, suggested itineraries, and key highlights of each island.

22.2 Transportation Between Islands

22.2.1 Flights

Inter-island flights are the quickest way to travel between the Canary Islands. Binter Canarias and Canaryfly are the primary airlines offering regular flights between the islands. Key routes include:

Tenerife North (TFN) to Gran Canaria (LPA): Approximately 30 minutes.

Lanzarote (ACE) to Fuerteventura (FUE): Approximately 35 minutes.

Gran Canaria (LPA) to La Palma (SPC): Approximately 50 minutes.

22.2.2 Ferries

Ferries are a scenic and popular option for island-hopping, allowing travelers to enjoy the sea and views of the islands. Major ferry operators include Fred. Olsen Express and Naviera Armas. Key routes include:

Tenerife to La Gomera: Approximately 1 hour.

Gran Canaria to Fuerteventura: Approximately 2.5 hours.

Lanzarote to Fuerteventura: Approximately 35 minutes.

22.2.3 Private Boat Charters

For a more personalized and flexible island-hopping experience, consider chartering a private boat. This option allows you to set your own schedule and explore smaller, less accessible locations.

22.3 Suggested Island-Hopping Itineraries

22.3.1 Classic Route: Tenerife, La Gomera, La Palma

Day 1-3: Tenerife

Mount Teide: Take a cable car ride and hike to the summit for breathtaking views.

Anaga Rural Park: Explore the lush laurel forests and scenic trails.

Santa Cruz de Tenerife: Visit the Auditorio de Tenerife and TEA Tenerife Espacio de las Artes.

Day 4-5: La Gomera

Garajonay National Park: Hike through ancient laurel forests.

San Sebastián: Explore the historic capital, including Torre del Conde and Casa de Colón.

Valle Gran Rey: Relax on the beaches and enjoy the tranquil atmosphere.

Day 6-8: La Palma

Caldera de Taburiente National Park: Hike through stunning volcanic landscapes.

Roque de los Muchachos: Visit the astronomical observatory and enjoy stargazing.

Santa Cruz de La Palma: Wander through the charming colonial town.

22.3.2 Volcanic Wonders: Lanzarote, Fuerteventura, Gran Canaria

Day 1-3: Lanzarote

Timanfaya National Park: Explore the volcanic landscapes and geothermal demonstrations.

Jameos del Agua: Visit the unique lava cave and cultural center designed by César Manrique.

La Geria: Tour the volcanic vineyards and sample local wines.

Day 4-5: Fuerteventura

Corralejo Natural Park: Discover the vast sand dunes and pristine beaches.

El Cotillo: Enjoy surfing and relaxing in this charming fishing village.

Betancuria: Explore the historic capital and its beautiful architecture.

Day 6-8: Gran Canaria

Roque Nublo: Hike to this iconic rock formation and enjoy panoramic views.

Maspalomas Dunes: Walk through the stunning sand dunes and visit the lighthouse.

Las Palmas: Explore the vibrant city, including the historic Vegueta district and the beach at Las Canteras.

22.3.3 Nature and Adventure: El Hierro, La Gomera, Tenerife

Day 1-2: El Hierro

La Restinga Marine Reserve: Dive or snorkel in one of Europe's best underwater sites.

Mirador de la Peña: Enjoy stunning views designed by César Manrique.

El Sabinar: Visit the wind-sculpted juniper trees.

Day 3-4: La Gomera

Garajonay National Park: Hike through the ancient forest.

Valle Gran Rey: Relax and explore this scenic valley.

Agulo: Visit one of the island's most picturesque villages.

Day 5-7: Tenerife

Mount Teide: Explore Spain's highest peak.

Anaga Rural Park: Discover the lush forests and trails.

La Laguna: Wander through this UNESCO World Heritage site.

22.4 Highlights of Each Island

22.4.1 Tenerife

Mount Teide: Spain's highest peak offers breathtaking views.

Loro Parque: A renowned animal park with diverse wildlife.

Santa Cruz: A vibrant city with cultural attractions and shopping.

22.4.2 Gran Canaria

Roque Nublo: Iconic rock formation and scenic hikes.

Maspalomas Dunes: Unique coastal sand dunes.

Las Palmas: Historic sites and beautiful beaches.

22.4.3 Lanzarote

Timanfaya National Park: Volcanic landscapes and geothermal activities.

César Manrique Foundation: Art and architecture blended with nature.

Papagayo Beaches: Pristine coves with clear waters.

22.4.4 Fuerteventura

Corralejo Natural Park: Vast dunes and stunning beaches.

Betancuria: Historic charm and cultural heritage.

Sotavento Beach: Ideal for windsurfing and kitesurfing.

22.4.5 La Palma

Caldera de Taburiente: Stunning national park with hiking trails.

Roque de los Muchachos: Astronomical observatories and stargazing.

Santa Cruz de La Palma: Colonial architecture and vibrant streets.

22.4.6 La Gomera

Garajonay National Park: Ancient laurel forests and hiking.

Valle Gran Rey: Scenic valley with beautiful beaches.

San Sebastián: Historical sites and charming town.

22.4.7 El Hierro

La Restinga Marine Reserve: Diving and marine life.

Mirador de la Peña: Panoramic views and César Manrique design.

El Sabinar: Unique, wind-sculpted juniper trees.

22.5 Practical Tips for Island-Hopping

22.5.1 Planning Your Itinerary

Research Each Island: Understand the key attractions and activities to prioritize your visits.

Allow Flexibility: Plan some extra time in case of transportation delays or spontaneous adventures.

Mix and Match: Combine different types of experiences, such as hiking, beach relaxation, and cultural exploration.

22.5.2 Booking Transportation

Flights: Book inter-island flights in advance for the best prices and availability.

Ferries: Check ferry schedules and book tickets ahead of time, especially during peak seasons.

Charters: If opting for a private boat charter, book early and confirm all details in advance.

22.5.3 Accommodation

Variety of Options: From luxury resorts to rural casas, choose accommodations that suit your travel style and budget.

Central Locations: Stay in central locations to minimize travel time to key attractions.

Book Ahead: Especially during high season, book your accommodations well in advance to secure the best options.

22.5.4 Packing Essentials

Light Layers: The climate varies across the islands, so pack light layers to accommodate different weather conditions.

Comfortable Shoes: Essential for hiking and exploring diverse terrains.

Swimwear and Sun Protection: For beach days and water activities, don't forget sunscreen, hats, and sunglasses.

Conclusion

Island-hopping in the Canary Islands offers a unique opportunity to experience the diverse beauty and cultural richness of the archipelago. With convenient transportation options and a wealth of attractions on each island, travelers can craft a personalized itinerary that showcases the best of what the Canary Islands have to offer. As we continue to explore the archipelago in the following chapters, the diverse offerings of each island will further illuminate the remarkable appeal of this destination.

Chapter 23: The Canary Islands for Couples: Romantic Getaways

23.1 Introduction to Romantic Getaways

The Canary Islands, with their stunning landscapes, beautiful beaches, and vibrant culture, provide the perfect setting for a romantic escape. Whether you're celebrating a honeymoon, anniversary, or simply seeking a romantic retreat, the Canary Islands offer a variety of experiences that cater to couples. This chapter explores the most romantic destinations, activities, and accommodations across the islands to help you plan an unforgettable getaway with your loved one.

23.2 Romantic Destinations

23.2.1 La Palma: The Green Island

La Palma, known as "La Isla Bonita" or "The Beautiful Island," is a paradise for couples seeking natural beauty and tranquility.

Caldera de Taburiente National Park: Hike through lush forests and enjoy breathtaking views of the caldera. A picnic by a secluded waterfall is a perfect romantic moment.

Roque de los Muchachos: Visit the highest point on the island for stunning sunsets and stargazing. The observatory offers guided tours for an educational and romantic experience.

Santa Cruz de La Palma: Stroll through the charming colonial streets, enjoy local cuisine, and explore the picturesque waterfront.

23.2.2 Lanzarote: The Volcanic Beauty

Lanzarote's unique volcanic landscapes and artistic touches by César Manrique make it a captivating destination for couples.

Timanfaya National Park: Explore the dramatic volcanic terrain and enjoy a geothermal-cooked meal at El Diablo restaurant.

Jameos del Agua: Experience the natural beauty and artistic design of this volcanic cave transformed into a cultural center by César Manrique.

Papagayo Beaches: Relax on the pristine beaches and swim in the crystal-clear waters of these secluded coves.

23.2.3 Tenerife: The Island of Eternal Spring

Tenerife offers a mix of adventure, relaxation, and cultural experiences, making it an ideal destination for couples.

Mount Teide: Take a cable car ride to Spain's highest peak and enjoy the panoramic views. Consider a sunset and stargazing tour for a truly magical experience.

La Laguna: Wander through the historic streets of this UNESCO World Heritage site, with its charming architecture and vibrant atmosphere.

Los Gigantes: Explore the dramatic cliffs and take a romantic boat tour to see dolphins and whales.

23.3 Romantic Activities

23.3.1 Sunset Cruises

A sunset cruise is a quintessential romantic experience in the Canary Islands, offering stunning views and a serene atmosphere.

Tenerife: Book a private yacht or catamaran tour departing from Costa Adeje or Los Gigantes to enjoy the sunset over the Atlantic Ocean.

Gran Canaria: Sail along the southern coast, with options for dinner and champagne on board.

23.3.2 Wine Tasting

Explore the unique wines of the Canary Islands with a romantic wine-tasting tour.

Lanzarote: Visit the volcanic vineyards of La Geria, such as Bodegas Rubicón or Bodegas El Grifo, for tastings and tours.

Tenerife: Explore the wine region of Tacoronte-Acentejo, with wineries like Bodegas Monje offering tastings and stunning views.

23.3.3 Spa Retreats

Indulge in a relaxing spa experience to rejuvenate and connect with your partner.

Gran Canaria: The Lopesan Costa Meloneras Resort offers luxurious spa treatments, thalassotherapy, and private couple's suites.

Tenerife: The Oriental Spa Garden at Hotel Botánico provides an array of wellness treatments, thermal circuits, and tranquil gardens.

23.3.4 Dining Experiences

Enjoy a romantic meal at some of the best dining spots in the Canary Islands.

El Rincón de Juan Carlos (Tenerife): This Michelin-starred restaurant in Los Gigantes offers an exquisite culinary experience with innovative dishes and impeccable service.

La Tegala (Lanzarote): Dine at this elegant restaurant with panoramic views, serving refined Canarian cuisine.

Amadores Beach Club (Gran Canaria): Enjoy a beachfront dining experience with gourmet cuisine and stunning ocean views.

23.4 Romantic Accommodations

23.4.1 Luxury Resorts

Stay at a luxurious resort that caters to couples with exclusive amenities and breathtaking views.

Bahia del Duque (Tenerife): This luxury resort in Costa Adeje offers elegant rooms, a world-class spa, and multiple fine dining options.

Gran Hotel Atlantis Bahía Real (Fuerteventura): Located in Corralejo, this resort features beautiful beachfront suites, a luxurious spa, and exquisite dining.

23.4.2 Boutique Hotels

Opt for a boutique hotel for a more intimate and personalized experience.

Hotel San Roque (Tenerife): A charming boutique hotel in Garachico, offering stylish rooms, a beautiful courtyard, and a rooftop terrace with ocean views.

La Casona de Yaiza (Lanzarote): A quaint boutique hotel in the village of Yaiza, featuring individually decorated rooms and a romantic atmosphere.

23.4.3 Rural Retreats

Escape to the countryside with a stay at a rural retreat, surrounded by nature and tranquility.

Hacienda de Abajo (La Palma): A historic hotel in Tazacorte, offering luxurious rooms, beautiful gardens, and a peaceful setting.

Casa León (Gran Canaria): A serene retreat in the mountains of Gran Canaria, providing stunning views, spa services, and gourmet dining.

23.5 Special Moments and Experiences

23.5.1 Stargazing

The clear skies and minimal light pollution of the Canary Islands make them one of the best destinations in the world for stargazing. Plan a romantic evening under the stars with a guided tour or simply find a secluded spot to enjoy the night sky.

Teide National Park (Tenerife): Join a stargazing tour with telescopes and expert guides to explore the wonders of the universe.

Roque de los Muchachos (La Palma): Visit the observatory and enjoy one of the best stargazing experiences in Europe.

23.5.2 Private Beach Picnics

Arrange a private beach picnic for a romantic and intimate experience.

Papagayo Beaches (Lanzarote): Find a secluded cove and set up a picnic with local delicacies and wine.

Playa de Las Teresitas (Tenerife): Enjoy a relaxing day on this beautiful beach with a picnic prepared by your hotel or a local deli.

23.5.3 Hot Air Balloon Rides

Experience the breathtaking landscapes of the Canary Islands from above with a hot air balloon ride.

Gran Canaria: Book a private hot air balloon tour for a unique perspective of the island's diverse scenery.

Tenerife: Enjoy a sunrise balloon ride over the stunning landscapes, creating unforgettable memories.

23.6 Practical Tips for Couples

23.6.1 Planning Your Itinerary

Balance Activities: Combine adventure and relaxation to cater to both your interests.

Book in Advance: Secure reservations for popular activities, dining, and accommodations to avoid disappointment.

Include Downtime: Allow for some downtime to relax and enjoy each other's company without a strict schedule.

23.6.2 Romantic Essentials

Pack Light: Bring versatile clothing for different activities and occasions.

Capture Memories: Take plenty of photos to remember your romantic getaway.

Personal Touches: Surprise your partner with thoughtful gestures, such as a special dinner or a small gift.

Conclusion

The Canary Islands offer an idyllic setting for a romantic getaway, with diverse landscapes, luxurious accommodations, and unforgettable experiences. Whether you're exploring volcanic landscapes, relaxing on pristine beaches, or indulging in fine dining, the Canary Islands provide the perfect backdrop for romance. As we continue to explore the archipelago in the following chapters, the diverse offerings of each island will further illuminate the remarkable appeal of this destination.

Chapter 24: Canary Islands for Families: Fun for All Ages

24.1 Introduction to Family-Friendly Travel

The Canary Islands are an excellent destination for family vacations, offering a wide range of activities and attractions that cater to all ages. From interactive museums and amusement parks to outdoor adventures and beautiful beaches, the archipelago provides endless opportunities for memorable family experiences. This chapter explores the best family-friendly activities across the Canary Islands, ensuring that every member of the family can enjoy a fantastic holiday.

24.2 Family-Friendly Beaches

24.2.1 Playa de Las Teresitas (Tenerife)

Playa de Las Teresitas is a man-made beach near Santa Cruz de Tenerife, featuring golden sand imported from the Sahara Desert. The calm waters and excellent facilities make it ideal for families.

Safe Swimming: The calm waters are perfect for young children and novice swimmers.

Amenities: Sun loungers, umbrellas, and beachside cafes enhance the visitor experience.

Shallow Waters: Ideal for children to play safely.

24.2.2 Playa del Inglés (Gran Canaria)

Playa del Inglés is one of the most popular beaches in Gran Canaria, offering a wide range of water sports and beach activities. The beach is well-equipped with amenities, including sun loungers, parasols, and restaurants.

Water Sports: Opportunities for windsurfing, jet skiing, and paddle boating.

Family-Friendly Facilities: Playgrounds and facilities for children.

Lifeguards: Ensuring safety for all swimmers.

24.2.3 Playa de Papagayo (Lanzarote)

Playa de Papagayo is a series of pristine beaches located in the Los Ajaches Natural Park. The calm, clear waters are perfect for swimming and snorkeling, making it a great spot for families.

Secluded Coves: Offer a sense of privacy and tranquility.

Crystal-Clear Waters: Ideal for snorkeling and exploring marine life.

Picnic Spots: Great for family outings and picnics.

24.3 Amusement and Theme Parks

24.3.1 Siam Park (Tenerife)

Siam Park is one of the largest and most popular water parks in Europe, located in Costa Adeje, Tenerife. The park features a Thai theme and offers a wide range of attractions, including:

The Dragon: A thrilling water slide that simulates zero gravity.

Siam Beach: A man-made beach with the world's largest artificial waves.

The Lost City: A water playground designed specifically for children, with shallow pools and smaller slides.

24.3.2 Loro Parque (Tenerife)

Loro Parque is a world-renowned animal park located in Puerto de la Cruz, Tenerife. The park is home to a diverse collection of animals, including parrots, dolphins, orcas, and gorillas. Highlights include:

Penguinarium: One of the world's largest indoor penguin exhibitions.

Orca Ocean: A spectacular show featuring orcas.

Planet Penguin: A state-of-the-art penguin habitat.

24.3.3 Aqualand Maspalomas (Gran Canaria)

Aqualand Maspalomas is a large water park in Gran Canaria, offering a variety of water slides, wave pools, and attractions for all ages. Popular features include:

Kamikaze: A high-speed water slide for thrill-seekers.

Pirate's Cove: A water playground with slides and splash zones for younger children.

Lazy River: A relaxing float along a winding river.

24.3.4 Rancho Texas Lanzarote Park (Lanzarote)

Rancho Texas Lanzarote Park is an animal and water park located near Puerto del Carmen, Lanzarote. The park offers a range of activities, including:

Animal Shows: Featuring birds of prey, sea lions, and parrots.

Splash Zone: A water playground with slides and pools.

Gold Mining: An interactive experience where kids can pan for "gold."

24.4 Interactive Museums and Educational Centers

24.4.1 Museo Elder de la Ciencia y la Tecnología (Gran Canaria)

The Elder Museum of Science and Technology in Las Palmas, Gran Canaria, offers interactive exhibits and hands-on activities that make learning fun for kids and adults alike. Highlights include:

Planetarium: A dome theater offering shows about the universe.

Robotics Area: Interactive exhibits showcasing the latest in robotics technology.

Science Workshops: Hands-on activities and experiments for children.

24.4.2 Museo de la Ciencia y el Cosmos (Tenerife)

The Museum of Science and the Cosmos in La Laguna, Tenerife, features interactive exhibits and educational displays that explore various scientific concepts. Highlights include:

Explora Room: An interactive space where kids can conduct experiments and learn through play.

Planetarium: Shows and presentations about space and astronomy.

Temporary Exhibits: Rotating displays on topics such as physics, biology, and technology.

24.4.3 Casa de los Balcones (Tenerife)

Located in La Orotava, Tenerife, the Casa de los Balcones is a historic house museum that offers a glimpse into traditional Canarian life. The museum features:

Traditional Crafts: Demonstrations of Canarian embroidery and lace-making.

Historic Architecture: Beautifully preserved wooden balconies and interior courtyards.

Interactive Exhibits: Hands-on activities for children, such as dressing in traditional costumes.

24.5 Outdoor Adventures

24.5.1 Camel Rides (Various Islands)

Camel rides are a popular activity in the Canary Islands, offering a unique way to explore the landscapes. Locations include:

Dunas de Maspalomas (Gran Canaria): Ride camels through the stunning sand dunes of Maspalomas.

Timanfaya National Park (Lanzarote): Experience a camel ride through the volcanic landscapes of the park.

24.5.2 Whale and Dolphin Watching (Various Islands)

The waters around the Canary Islands are home to several species of whales and dolphins. Family-friendly boat tours offer the chance to see these magnificent creatures up close. Popular departure points include:

Los Cristianos (Tenerife): Tours often spot pilot whales and bottlenose dolphins.

Puerto Rico (Gran Canaria): Regular sightings of various dolphin species and occasional whales.

La Palma: Known for its clear waters and frequent dolphin sightings.

24.5.3 Hiking and Nature Walks (Various Islands)

Many of the islands offer family-friendly hiking trails and nature walks that showcase their natural beauty.

Garajonay National Park (La Gomera): The park offers several easy trails suitable for families, including the Bosque del Cedro walk.

Anaga Rural Park (Tenerife): Family-friendly trails such as the Path of the Senses offer short, accessible hikes through lush forests.

Caldera de Taburiente National Park (La Palma): The park features various trails, including the easy walk to the Cascada de los Colores waterfall.

24.6 Animal Parks and Zoos

24.6.1 Palmitos Park (Gran Canaria)

Palmitos Park is a botanical garden and zoo located in the south of Gran Canaria. The park features a wide variety of animals, including birds, reptiles, and mammals. Highlights include:

Dolphinarium: Home to several dolphins, with daily shows and interactive experiences.

Bird Shows: Featuring exotic birds such as parrots and birds of prey.

Orchid House: A beautiful collection of orchids and other tropical plants.

24.6.2 Oasis Park (Fuerteventura)

Oasis Park is a large zoo and botanical garden located in La Lajita, Fuerteventura. The park offers a range of attractions, including:

Animal Shows: Featuring sea lions, birds of prey, and parrots.

Safari Experience: A guided tour through the park's savanna area, home to giraffes, zebras, and other African animals.

Camel Rides: A unique way to explore the park's landscape.

24.6.3 Jungle Park (Tenerife)

Jungle Park is a zoo and adventure park located in Arona, Tenerife. The park features a variety of animals, as well as adventure attractions such as:

Bird of Prey Show: Featuring eagles, hawks, and vultures.

Penguin Exhibit: A state-of-the-art habitat for penguins.

Bob Jungle: A toboggan run through the park's lush landscape.

24.7 Interactive Farms and Botanical Gardens

24.7.1 Finca Canarias Aloe Vera (Various Islands)

Finca Canarias Aloe Vera offers guided tours of aloe vera plantations across several islands, including Tenerife, Gran Canaria, and Lanzarote. Visitors can learn about the cultivation and processing of aloe vera and sample various aloe vera products.

24.7.2 Cactus Garden (Lanzarote)

The Cactus Garden in Guatiza, Lanzarote, is a beautifully landscaped garden featuring over 1,000 species of cacti. Designed by César Manrique, the garden offers a unique and educational experience for families.

24.7.3 La Granja Verde (Gran Canaria)

La Granja Verde is an interactive farm located in the north of Gran Canaria. The farm offers a range of activities, including:

Animal Encounters: Meet and feed various farm animals, including goats, pigs, and chickens.

Workshops: Learn about traditional farming practices and participate in activities such as cheese-making and bread-baking.

Nature Walks: Explore the farm's gardens and orchards.

24.8 Adventure Parks and Zip Lines

24.8.1 Forestal Park (Tenerife)

Forestal Park is an adventure park located in Las Lagunetas, Tenerife. The park offers a range of activities, including:

Zip Lines: A series of thrilling zip lines through the forest.

Rope Courses: Various courses of differing difficulty levels, suitable for both children and adults.

Climbing Walls: Indoor and outdoor climbing walls for all ages.

24.8.2 GrancAventura (Gran Canaria)

GrancAventura is an adventure park located in Arucas, Gran Canaria. The park features a variety of activities, including:

Zip Lines: Multiple zip lines that offer exciting rides through the park.

Obstacle Courses: A range of courses designed for different age groups and skill levels.

Archery: An archery range where visitors can learn and practice archery skills.

24.9 Family-Friendly Festivals and Events

24.9.1 Carnival (Various Islands)

The Carnival is a major event across the Canary Islands, with colorful parades, music, and dance. Family-friendly activities include:

Children's Parades: Special parades and events designed for children.

Costume Contests: Fun contests where kids can show off their costumes.

Family Zones: Areas with games, rides, and entertainment for children.

24.9.2 Fiestas de San Juan (Various Islands)

The Fiestas de San Juan are celebrated across the Canary Islands, marking the summer solstice. Family-friendly activities include:

Bonfires: Beach bonfires and fireworks.

Nighttime Swims: Traditional midnight swims in the ocean.

Live Music and Dancing: Festivities often include live music and dance performances.

24.9.3 Día de Canarias (Various Islands)

Día de Canarias is celebrated on May 30th and includes a variety of family-friendly events, such as:

Traditional Music and Dance: Performances showcasing Canarian folk music and dance.

Cultural Workshops: Activities where children can learn about Canarian crafts and traditions.

Food Stalls: Sample local dishes and sweets.

24.10 Practical Tips for Families

24.10.1 Planning Your Itinerary

Balance Activities: Mix high-energy activities with relaxation time to keep everyone happy.

Include Downtime: Allow for breaks and naps, especially for younger children.

Plan Ahead: Book popular attractions and accommodations in advance to avoid disappointment.

24.10.2 Packing Essentials

Comfortable Clothing: Pack for a variety of activities and weather conditions.

Sun Protection: Bring sunscreen, hats, and sunglasses to protect against the strong sun.

Snacks and Water: Keep snacks and water on hand for outings and day trips.

24.10.3 Safety and Health

Stay Hydrated: Ensure everyone drinks plenty of water, especially during outdoor activities.

First Aid Kit: Pack a basic first aid kit for minor injuries and illnesses.

Know the Rules: Familiarize yourself with local safety regulations, such as beach flags and hiking guidelines.

Conclusion

The Canary Islands offer a wealth of family-friendly activities that cater to all ages and interests. From amusement parks and interactive museums to outdoor adventures and cultural festivals, there is something for every member of the family to enjoy. By exploring the diverse attractions and activities across the islands, families can create lasting memories and experience the unique charm and hospitality of the Canary Islands. As we continue to explore the archipelago in the following chapters, the diverse offerings of each island will further illuminate the remarkable appeal of this destination.

Chapter 25: Practical Information for Travelers to the Canary Islands

25.1 Introduction

Planning a trip to the Canary Islands involves more than just deciding on activities and accommodations. It's essential to be well-informed about the practical aspects of travel to ensure a smooth and enjoyable experience. This chapter provides detailed information on travel essentials, including visas and entry requirements, transportation options, health and safety tips, local customs, and useful travel tips for navigating the Canary Islands.

25.2 Visas and Entry Requirements

25.2.1 Entry Requirements for EU Citizens

Citizens of the European Union (EU) and Schengen Area countries do not require a visa to enter the Canary Islands, as Spain is part of the Schengen Agreement. Travelers need a valid passport or national ID card.

25.2.2 Entry Requirements for Non-EU Citizens

Non-EU citizens may require a visa to enter Spain and the Canary Islands, depending on their nationality. Travelers should check the specific requirements for their country of origin.

Visa-Free Travel: Citizens of some countries, such as the United States, Canada, Australia, and New Zealand, can enter the Canary Islands for short stays (up to 90 days) without a visa.

Visa Applications: Travelers from countries that require a visa must apply at the Spanish consulate or embassy in their home country before their trip.

25.2.3 Health and Travel Insurance

While health insurance is not mandatory for entry, it is highly recommended to have travel insurance that covers medical expenses, trip cancellations, and other potential issues. EU citizens can use the

European Health Insurance Card (EHIC) for emergency medical treatment.

25.3 Transportation Options

25.3.1 Getting to the Canary Islands

25.3.1.1 By Air

The most common way to reach the Canary Islands is by air. The archipelago has several international airports:

Tenerife South Airport (TFS): Located in the south of Tenerife, serving many international and domestic flights.

Gran Canaria Airport (LPA): Located near Las Palmas, offering extensive connections to Europe and beyond.

Lanzarote Airport (ACE): Serving the island of Lanzarote with numerous international flights.

Fuerteventura Airport (FUE): Connecting Fuerteventura with many European destinations.

25.3.1.2 By Sea

Ferries operate between mainland Spain and the Canary Islands, although this option is less common due to the long travel time (approximately 36 hours).

25.3.2 Getting Around the Islands

25.3.2.1 Public Transportation

Public transportation is efficient and affordable, particularly on the larger islands.

Buses: Known as "guaguas" in the Canary Islands, buses are the primary mode of public transportation, with extensive networks in Tenerife, Gran Canaria, and other islands.

Trams: Tenerife offers a tram service between Santa Cruz and La Laguna.

25.3.2.2 Car Rentals

Renting a car is a convenient way to explore the islands at your own pace, especially for visiting remote areas and natural attractions.

Rental Agencies: Major international and local car rental companies operate at airports and in major towns.

Driving Tips: Drive on the right-hand side, and be prepared for narrow and winding roads in rural areas.

25.3.2.3 Taxis and Ride-Sharing

Taxis are widely available, and ride-sharing services like Uber and Cabify operate in some areas.

Taxis: Metered and reliable, taxis are a good option for short distances and airport transfers.

Ride-Sharing: Available in major cities and tourist areas, offering an alternative to traditional taxis.

25.3.3 Inter-Island Travel

25.3.3.1 Flights

Inter-island flights are the quickest way to travel between the islands, with frequent services provided by Binter Canarias and Canaryfly.

25.3.3.2 Ferries

Ferries are a scenic and popular option for island-hopping, with services operated by Fred. Olsen Express and Naviera Armas.

25.4 Health and Safety

25.4.1 Health Services

The Canary Islands have a well-developed healthcare system with public and private hospitals and clinics.

Emergency Services: Dial 112 for emergency medical assistance.

Pharmacies: Widely available in towns and cities, with many open 24 hours.

25.4.2 Safety Tips

The Canary Islands are generally safe for travelers, but it's always wise to take precautions.

Personal Safety: Be aware of your surroundings, especially in crowded areas, to avoid pickpocketing.

Beach Safety: Pay attention to beach safety flags and warnings, as currents can be strong.

Hiking Safety: Stay on marked trails, carry sufficient water, and inform someone of your hiking plans.

25.5 Local Customs and Etiquette

25.5.1 Language

Spanish is the official language of the Canary Islands. While English is widely spoken in tourist areas, learning a few basic Spanish phrases can be helpful and appreciated.

25.5.2 Greetings and Social Etiquette

Greetings: A handshake is common when meeting someone for the first time. Friends and acquaintances may greet each other with a kiss on both cheeks.

Dining Etiquette: Wait for the host to begin eating, and use "buen provecho" (enjoy your meal) as a polite gesture.

Tipping: Tipping is appreciated but not obligatory. A 5-10% tip in restaurants and rounding up the fare for taxi drivers is customary.

25.5.3 Dress Code

Casual Wear: Light, casual clothing is suitable for most occasions, especially in tourist areas.

Beachwear: Swimwear is appropriate for the beach but not for town centers or restaurants.

Evening Wear: Smart casual attire is recommended for dining out or attending events.

25.6 Useful Travel Tips

25.6.1 Currency and Banking

Currency: The Euro (€) is the official currency.

ATMs and Credit Cards: Widely available and accepted. Inform your bank of your travel plans to avoid card issues.

Exchange Rates: Check rates before exchanging money to get the best deal.

25.6.2 Internet and Communication

Internet Access: Wi-Fi is widely available in hotels, restaurants, and cafes. Public Wi-Fi hotspots are common in tourist areas.

Mobile Phones: Ensure your phone is unlocked and compatible with European networks. Purchasing a local SIM card can be cost-effective for data and calls.

25.6.3 Weather and Best Time to Visit

Climate: The Canary Islands enjoy a subtropical climate with mild temperatures year-round. Summers are warm and winters are mild, making them a great destination any time of year.

Best Time to Visit: Spring and autumn offer pleasant weather and fewer crowds, while summer is popular for beach vacations.

25.6.4 Electricity and Plugs

Voltage: The standard voltage is 230V.

Plugs: The Canary Islands use Type C and Type F plugs. Bring a universal adapter if your devices use different plugs.

Conclusion

Being well-prepared with practical information can greatly enhance your travel experience in the Canary Islands. Understanding entry requirements, transportation options, health and safety tips, and local customs will help ensure a smooth and enjoyable trip. As we conclude this guide to the Canary Islands, we hope the detailed insights provided in each chapter have inspired and equipped you for an unforgettable adventure in this beautiful archipelago. Enjoy your journey and embrace the unique charm and hospitality of the Canary Islands!

9 798822 765927